Securitizing Immigration

Palgrave Studies in International Relations Series

Palgrave Studies in International Relations, produced in association with the ECPR Standing Group for International Relations, will provide students and scholars with the best theoretically-informed scholarship on the global issues of our time. Edited by Knud Erik Jørgensen and Audie Klotz, this new book series will comprise cutting-edge monographs and edited collections which bridge schools of thought and cross the boundaries of conventional fields of study.

Titles include

Barry Buzan and Ana Gonzalez-Pelaez (*editors*)
INTERNATIONAL SOCIETY AND THE MIDDLE EAST
English School Theory at the Regional Level

Cornelia Navari (*editor*)
THEORISING INTERNATIONAL SOCIETY
English School Methods

Robbie Shilliam
GERMAN THOUGHT AND INTERNATIONAL RELATIONS
The Rise and Fall of a Liberal Project

Rens van Munster
SECURITIZING IMMIGRATION
The Politics of Risk in the EU

Palgrave Studies In International Relations Series
Series Standing Order ISBN 978–0230–20063–0

You can receive future titles in this series as they are published by placing a standing order. Please contact your bookseller or, in case of difficulty, write to us at the address below with your name and address, the title of the series and the ISBN quoted above.

Customer Services Department, Macmillan Distribution Ltd, Houndmills, Basingstoke, Hampshire RG21 6XS, England

Securitizing Immigration

The Politics of Risk in the EU

Rens van Munster
Senior Researcher, Research Unit on Defence and Security, Danish Institute for International Studies, Denmark

palgrave
macmillan

First published 2009 by
PALGRAVE MACMILLAN

Palgrave Macmillan in the UK is an imprint of Macmillan Publishers Limited, registered in England, company number 785998, of Houndmills, Basingstoke, Hampshire RG21 6XS.

Palgrave Macmillan in the US is a division of St Martin's Press LLC, 175 Fifth Avenue, New York, NY 10010.

Palgrave Macmillan is the global academic imprint of the above companies and has companies and representatives throughout the world.

Palgrave® and Macmillan® are registered trademarks in the United States, the United Kingdom, Europe and other countries.

ISBN: 978–0–230–20006–7 hardback

This book is printed on paper suitable for recycling and made from fully managed and sustained forest sources. Logging, pulping and manufacturing processes are expected to conform to the environmental regulations of the country of origin.

A catalogue record for this book is available from the British Library.

A catalog record for this book is available from the Library of Congress.

10 9 8 7 6 5 4 3 2 1
18 17 16 15 14 13 12 11 10 09

Printed and bound in Great Britain by
CPI Antony Rowe, Chippenham and Eastbourne

Contents

List of Figures

Figures

Acknowledgements

This book builds on PhD research completed at the University of Southern Denmark, Odense. I would like to thank the Department of Political Science for providing a generous research environment. I would also like to express thanks to my colleagues and friends at the department for their academic and practical support. In 2003–2004, I was awarded a one-year Marie Curie Fellowship in International Political Community by the Department of International Politics at the University of Wales, Aberystwyth. It was a huge privilege to spend a year at what must be one of the most vibrant environments for IR scholars. I would also like to thank Claudia Aradau, Didier Bigo, Ken Booth, Jenny Edkins, Stefano Guzzini, Finn Laursen, Andrew Linklater, Debbie Lisle, Cian O'Driscoll, Columba Peoples, Jens Ringsmose, Christilla Roederer-Rynning, Sten Rynning, Casper Sylvest, Nick Vaughan-Williams, Mike Williams and Nick Wheeler for taking their time to discuss and comment on some of the ideas that are part of this book. Thanks to two anonymous reviewers for their extensive and useful comments. Amy Lankester-Owen and Gemma d'Arcy Hughes from Palgrave patiently assisted during the production process. Stefan de la Puente Kristiansen and Toke Lassen compiled the index.

A few people deserve special mention. As my teachers at the University of Twente, Wouter Werner and Jaap de Wilde were my first encounter with the field of International Relations theory. Their engagement and enthusiasm for IR proved to be contagious. I am delighted that today we are good colleagues and friends. Alistair Shepherd read drafts of various chapters and showed me that epistemological differences need not stand in the way of good discussions. Knud-Erik Jørgensen read an earlier version of this manuscript and encouraged me to turn it into a book project for this Palgrave series. Anna Leander also commented on an earlier version of this manuscript. Her sharp suggestions and advice were always on the spot. To Jef Huysmans I owe more than he is probably aware of himself or wants to take credit for. Not only did he comment on an earlier version of this manuscript, but his work and generous feed-back over the past years has been very influential for the development of my thinking about security. I am sure many other younger scholars feel the same way. Thanks to Tanja Aalberts for being my constructivist partner in crime at more methodological courses than either of us cares to remember. Many megabytes of real-time frustration, joy and encouragement have been sent back and forth between our respective computers – I hope these exchanges were as rewarding for her as they were for me. I would especially like to thank Ton and Tineke van Munster for their incalculable support and encouragement over all those years. I truly could not wish for better parents. Finally, I want to thank my partner Anna Christina Riisager for risking her life with me. Cheerful, loving and intelligent, she constantly reminds me of life's true priorities. Every day, she makes Denmark feel like home.

List of Acronyms

AFSJ	Area of Freedom, Security and Justice
AHWGI	Ad Hoc Working Group on Immigration
CCTV	Closed Circuit Television
CIREA	Centre for Information, Reflection and Exchange on Asylum Matters
CIREFI	Centre for Information, Reflection and Exchange on the Crossing of Borders and Immigration
CIS	Customs Information Database
COREPER	Committee of Permanent Representatives
DG	Directorate General
ECJ	European Court of Justice
EP	European Parliament
EU	European Union
HIG	Horizontal Information Group
HLWG	High Level Working Group on Immigration
IGC	Intergovernmental Conference
JHA	Justice and Home Affairs
RSC	Robmarine Shipping Consultants
SCIFA	Strategic Committee for Immigration, Frontiers and Asylum
SIS	Schengen Information System
TEC	Treaty Establishing the European Communities
TEU	Treaty on European Union [Maastricht Treaty]
Trevi	Terrorisme, Radicalisme, Extrémisme et Violence Internationale
UN	United Nations
VIS	Visa Identification System

1
Introduction

Immigration and European integration

This book seeks to account for the developments whereby immigrants into the EU have acquired the politically salient status of 'risky' and 'dangerous' when only a few decades ago they were considered a peripheral question to the project of European integration. It asks how it is possible that the issue of immigration has been increasingly rendered visible as a security issue on the level of the EU and not as, say, a humanitarian or economic issue.

At first sight, this puzzle does not appear a puzzle at all. Politicians, policy-makers and the media often explain the view of immigrants as a source of insecurity by pointing out the increased number of immigrants and asylum-seekers during the early 1990s. However, such numbers prove little by themselves and there is no obvious connection between the number of immigrants and the frame of security. During the 1950s and the 1960s, for example, Western European states recruited large numbers of immigrants for economic purposes without triggering any of the security concerns that characterize the current debate on immigration. To the contrary, in Western European countries such as France, Germany, the Netherlands and Belgium, the policy-making elites considered foreign labour a useful means to promote economic development and socio-political stability.

Interestingly, the undocumented status of immigrants was of minor concern only. Whereas today the 'fight' against 'illegal' immigration is one of the spear points of EU immigration policy, for a long time the issue of legality was subordinate to concerns about labour market gaps. Actually, the unregulated status of immigrants was viewed as an opportunity to exploit immigrant labour. As the former French Minister for Social Affairs, Jean Marie Jeanney, argued in 1966: 'Illegal immigration has its uses, for if we rightly adhere to the regulations and international agreements we would perhaps be short of labour' (cited in Geddes 2003: 53). In France, therefore, a residence permit could be obtained without a work permit and foreign labour was mainly recruited by the private sector outside the influence of public authorities. Furthermore, many immigrants living in France during the 1950s and 1960s did so without the appropriate identity documents (Hollifield 1994: 146). Although countries such as Germany and the Netherlands were generally more inclined to regulate the status of immigrants through the signing of recruitment agreements, these usually merely formalized and regulated the flows of immigrants that were already arriving in these countries before such agreements were concluded.[1]

Within the context of European integration, the question of third country immigration was not a topic of heated policy debate either. For a long time immigration was considered to be a national matter and the EU only had an indirect impact on immigration policies through the promotion of free movement of member states nationals. For example, Council Regulation 1612/68 on free movement within the EU distinguishes explicitly between EU-nationals and non-EU nationals, stating that vacancies should only be offered to third country nationals if no EU-nationals could fill those vacancies (for a discussion, see Ugur 1995: 976). While the 1968 Regulation certainly was discriminatory in origin, this was not part of a deliberate attempt to 'fight' immigration.[2] Rather, immigration remained a peripheral question which was only 'considered in the context of social and economic rights and the construction of an integrated labour market in which workers could freely move between Member States' (Huysmans 2000a: 755). Indeed, until the early 1980s European cooperation on immigration was mainly channelled through the United Nations (UN) and the Council of Europe rather than the EU (Lavenex 2001).

This changed dramatically during the 1980s and 1990s, when immigration policy became increasingly Europeanized as part of Justice and Home Affairs (JHA) which has played a crucial role in the development of the EU as an Area of Freedom, Security and Justice (AFSJ). Immigration is predominantly framed and managed as a high-ranking security issue to the Union, the internal market and the freedom enjoyed by

EU-citizens. The current securitization of immigration in the EU provides an intriguing lens through which to explore the constitution of a European polity. Since immigration generally invokes thorny political questions of identity, loyalty, access and voice, what does it mean to interpret immigration as a security problem? How does the invocation of 'security' structure social relations within the EU, between the EU and its external environment? And how does it impact upon the distinction between EU-citizens and third country nationals? In which ways do security practices draw the boundaries of the EU?

These are the central questions of this book. More specifically, it pursues three related objectives. First, it unpacks the political and bureaucratic processes and struggles that drove the process by means of which immigration and asylum arose as security questions in the European integration process. In addition, this book draws out the specific governmental logic of insecurity – i.e. liberal risk administration – which these bureaucratic and political processes inscribed in European migration policy (and other justice and home affairs policy areas) in the European Union. The governmental logic of liberal risk management can help us understand the paradoxical existence of the EU as a liberal polity on the one hand and the renewed importance of exceptional and security practices in this polity on the other. Finally, this book explores forms of belonging that do not rely on the exclusionary measures of security around which the EU is constituted as an area of freedom, security and justice.

The securitization of immigration in the EU

In an attempt to show how immigration has been rendered visible as a security issue on the level of the EU (and not as, say, a humanitarian or economic issue), this book introduces some of the conceptual debates that are taking place within security studies into the discipline of European integration. This aims to introduce a constructivist agenda of threat construction into EU Studies. While constructivism is of course not an unknown species within the field of European integration (see Jørgensen 1997; Christiansen, Jørgensen et al. 2001; Walters and Haahr 2005), European integration theory has nevertheless tended to explain the emergence of a European politics of internal security as an objective response to sources of insecurity (Knelangen 2001; Mitsilegas, Monar et al. 2003; Müller 2003; Occhipinti 2003).

As a result, European integration theories have been unable to account for the Europeanization of immigration as a security issue. For instance, the liberal intergovernmentalist understanding of the EU as a two-level game of national preference formation and international bargaining does not take us far in explaining the shift towards a more security-oriented understanding of immigration. In fact, such theories would have us expect the opposite. As Geddes puts it, 'tendencies towards expansive immigration policies are actually a structural characteristic of liberal states because the advocates of expansion, such as business interests, are better organised and have the ear of government, compared with the opponents of immigration, who are not and do not' (see also Hollifield 1992; Freeman 1995; Geddes 2000: 23).[3] Despite the expectation that liberal polities tend to opt for expansive policies immigration policies, the EU has however developed an increasingly restrictive regime.

Also analyses that rely upon functionalist arguments of spill-over have a hard time accounting for the security framing of immigration. According to this theory, the abolition of internal borders for economic reasons requires cooperation in the field of security as open borders were thought to also facilitate criminal and illegal movement.[4] Although, intuitively, this argument may sound appealing, its logic is seriously flawed. First, there is no statistical evidence to support the thesis that the abolishment of internal borders increases outside pressures.[5] Second, this explanation puts too much emphasis on the border. On the one hand, it wrongly assumes that people only decide to move when borders are abolished. On the other, it greatly overestimates the effectiveness of border as a control instrument.[6]

Third, the view that security measures cover security deficits created by economic cooperation fits uncomfortably with the insight that important compensatory measures such as Schengen temporally *preceded* the large inflow of asylum-seekers in the early 1990s.[7] Crucially, this reverses the claim that compensatory measures were a *reaction* to outside pressures (see Chapter 2 for a more detailed analysis). Finally, and most importantly, the spill-over argument does not tell us why immigration should be included as a threat alongside terrorism, organized crime and drugs trafficking. More generally, the specific form, scope and extent of security cooperation cannot be adequately accounted for by functionalist reasoning. Just how much security is needed? Which actors should do the securing? Which procedures, actors and institutions should be established to deal with threats? And who decides what kinds of threats require responses in the first place?

Despite the prevalence of functionalist arguments in European integration theory, the connection between free movement and internal security is thus far than self-explanatory. This book suggests that the constructivist focus on the bureaucratic and political processes of threat construction is a more suitable framework for analysis. Building upon the Copenhagen School's theoretical framework of securitization, this book proposes to explore the process of securitization as the interplay between bureaucratic framing and political negotiations. Where the security literature often analyses the political level as simply legitimating what happens in bureaucratic processes, this book points out that politics can also open up bureaucratic sedimentation.

In its broadest sense, the concept of securitization implies that threats are not out there but constructed by social actors. Drawing on the linguistic theory of Austin and Searle, the Copenhagen School defines security as a speech act:

> 'Security' is thus a self-referential practice, because it is in this practice that the issue becomes a security issue – not necessarily because a real existential threat exists but because the issue is presented as such a threat ... The process of security is what in language theory is called a speech act. It is not interesting as a sign referring to something more real; it is the utterance itself that is the act. By saying the words, something is done (like betting, giving a promise, naming a ship) (Buzan, Wæver et al. 1998: 24, 26).

The 'securityness' of immigration cannot be assessed outside its discursive production. But from which authoritative position can security legitimately be enunciated? Bigo (1996, 2001) has suggested that the capacity to speak security should be located in the practices of bureaucratic experts. In modern Western societies the locus of security decisions is not the property of individual political actors, but located within the expert regimes of bureaucratic systems. To privilege the speech of political actors therefore risks ignoring the more mundane and routine-like processes of securitization which take place on an every-day basis.

Integrating empirical analysis of the securitization of migration in the European Union with theoretical interventions in the literature on

European integration, this book also contributes to conceptual developments in security studies. Considering the political and bureaucratic level as mutually constitutive, this book proposes a slightly different position than the one suggested by Bigo and his colleagues. On the one hand, it agrees with Bigo and his colleagues that the capacity to speak security is often located in specific institutionalized environments. Security experts make sense of and interact with the world on the basis of their professional self-understanding as those responsible for the regulation and management of dangers in society. In this sense, the term 'risk', with its institutional and bureaucratic connotations of management, seems more appropriate than the more dramatic notion of security.

On the other hand, this study shows it would be wrong to focus on the bureaucratic level alone. While Bigo may be right that the political power to take decisions is not terribly interesting if it is considered in isolation from the security professionals' power to determine the security agenda, political decision-making is still relevant in as far as it translates bureaucratic discourses into budgets, institution-building and decision-making. Some sort of interplay between the bureaucratic level of risk management and the political level of security-speak is always present. Although the main security dynamics are located at the bureaucratic level, the focus on bureaucratic practices alone risks ending up with a somewhat conspirational understanding of security as the increasing colonization of everyday life by security professionals such as the police, military and intelligence services. This 'doom scenario' of security experts taking over the world is reflected, for example, in Aradau's (Aradau 2001: 5) somewhat deterministic statement that we today live in a 'society at the mercy of a bureaucratized network which thrives on unsolvable security issues'. As I will show in Chapters 3 to 5, the political level often plays an important role in either authorizing, legitimizing, justifying, thwarting, dislocating or upsetting the enunciations of security professionals (see Figure 1.1).

Within the context of the EU, the intergovernmental conferences in particular are important elements in the securitization process because of their potential to introduce a sense of contingency in the routine practices and discourses that are played out on the EU-level. In intergovernmental conferences (as in elections), the normal or regular way of doing things is, at least to a certain degree, suspended. Intergovernmental bargains have the potential to open up

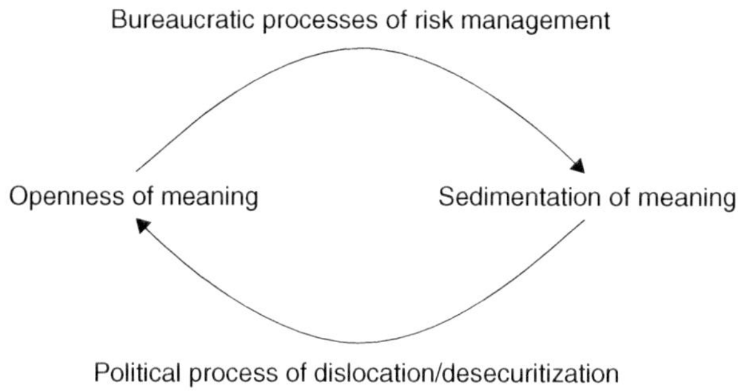

Figure 1.1 Securitization: The bureaucratic and political level

the reality of bureaucratic routines, while creating room for manoeuvre for bureaucratic agents to articulate and mobilize new discourses and knowledges. Political negotiations can relocate the authority to govern and manage immigration to professional contexts that are not concerned with threat management, such as development workers, foreign affairs officials or labour market experts. Thus, even if not everybody agrees with the view that intergovernmental negotiations represent the 'constitutional moments', 'grand bargains' or 'big bangs' of the integration process, few would claim that they do not matter at all.

In sum, by arguing that the functional sector of security and threat management is connected to the intergovernmental process of political bargaining, this book seeks to explain the securitization of immigration from a combined bureaucratic-politics perspective.

Security and the political: Liberalism, mobility, abjection

A second reason for bringing the concept of securitization into European Studies concerns the relation between security and the political. The framing of immigration in terms of security has a profound impact upon central political issues such as EU-citizenship, the relationship between EU-nationals with third country nationals and the ways in which the EU relates to its external environment. As Huysmans (2006: 13) rightly notes, 'securitization in both its discursive and technocratic dimensions bears upon the more general question of the political identity of the EU.' Unfortunately, within European Studies, the constitutive relationship between security and the political is generally ignored. The EU is regarded as a pre-constituted entity with the capability to deploy a range of means and instruments to attain security. Yet, this ignores that the management of a security situation is at the same time also a founding practice for the community. Practices of security produce internal order by distributing trust between members of the community while relegating indeterminacy, fear and anarchy outside the social order. The risk management of immigration is a particular politics of belonging that distributes trust and fear.

Generally, within security studies, security has been understood as a *realist* practice that constitutes the political through the staging of an existential threat that is claimed to threaten the survival of a community.[8] The realist understanding of security as a practice that integrates individuals according to the friend/enemy distinction also defines the Copenhagen School's speech act theory. According to the Copenhagen school, a securitizing act can be defined in the following way: 'If by means of an argument about the priority and urgency of an existential threat the securitizing actor has managed to break free of procedures or rules he or she would otherwise be bound by, we are witnessing a case of securitization' (Buzan, Wæver et al. 1998: 25). Through a securitizing act an actor thus tries to elevate an issue from the realm of low politics (bounded by democratic rules and decision-making procedures) to the realm of high politics, war and national security. It is through the move towards this war-like opposition that actors establish their identity vis-à-vis an existential enemy (Schmitt 1996: 39). Embedded within a vision of the political as an exceptional domain, the Copenhagen School thus understands security as a binary, zero-sum game of identity-formation that establishes an intense and particularly forceful relationship between two opposing groups (Huysmans 1998; Williams 2003).

Yet, the securitization of immigration in the EU does not operate according to the sovereign *logic of war* that brings death into play through the staging of an existential threat. It does not seek to integrate free individuals into a political community according to the principle of Schmittian realism, but integrates EU citizens within the EU-order through the promotion of freedom qua mobility. While Huysmans (2006: 102) has suggested that the relationship between freedom and security is at the heart of all modern politics, this book argues that 'governing through freedom' is better understood as a specific *liberal* mode of governing. Only within a liberal rationality is freedom viewed as an indispensable element in administering a population. As Gordon argues: 'Liberty is the circumambient medium of governmental action: disrespect of liberty is not simply an illegitimate violation of rights, but an ignorance of how to govern' (Gordon 1991: 20). Freedom is to be promoted, encouraged, harnessed and guided.

Within the governmental rationality of the EU, individuals are therefore not only free to move, they are also expected to do so – hence the great importance the EU attaches to harmonization, which basically is a process of deterritorialization with the aim of ensuring that the mobility of capital, goods and persons within the EU is unimpeded by national economic, political or social constraints (Barry 2001). Crucially, however, the exercise of mobility within the EU does not just depend upon facilitating measures that seek to establish the optimal conditions under which individuals actively start governing their own conduct of freedom; it also depends on the governance of what Huysmans has called the improper and irresponsible exercise of freedom (see Huysmans 2004a; van Munster and Sterkx 2005). Taking point of departure in the independent, autonomous liberal self as the norm against which the behavioural habits of individuals and groups is measured, calculated and, when necessary, corrected (Dean 2002), liberal governance divides between autonomous subjects and deviant, abject beings. As Hindess argues, in liberalism

> we should also expect to find the development of routines for dealing with deviant cases: those families thought to provide a poor environment for the care and, especially, the socialization of children, immigrants who may not know the language, long-term unemployed people in danger of losing the habits of discipline required for regular employment, unemployed youth who may never have learned those habits, and so on ... In place of the pervasive effects of discipline, an equally pervasive government of freedom is invoked, to similar effect (Hindess 1996: 130, 131).

Freedom, then, is not just something to be let loose and canalized in the internal market; it is also something to be managed through the constant monitoring of activities that are identified as undermining mobility. Within the liberal rationality of governing security reappears as a technique for regulating the deviant conduct of freedom (Huysmans 2006). Figure 1.2 summarizes the differences between a political realist understanding of security and a liberal logic of security.

	Political realism	*Liberalism*
Representation of threat	Friend/enemy opposition; personification of the enemy	Friend/enemy continuum; impersonal correlation of factors liable to produce risk
Measures/strategy	Exceptional measures that bypass normal political procedures; measures counteract existential threat	Normal measures such as surveillance and risk profiling; measures contribute to the social control of larger populations
Objective	Elimination of threat; the elimination of a threat secures the collective survival of a socio-political order	Freedom; management of risks secures the circulation of goods, persons and capital

Figure 1.2 Two logics of security: Political realism v. liberalism

The focus on the governmental logic of liberalism does not imply that the realist logic of war has no validity at all for understanding how security operates in the EU. A brief glance at the metaphors deployed in discourses on immigration – the 'war' or 'fight' against immigration; 'Fortress' Europe; the 'combating' of immigration; 'flanking' measures; 'frontline' states – all bear witness to the continuing importance of the language game of war in structuring social relations between the EU and third country nationals. Nevertheless, on the level of practices (rather than speech) security has become more and more de-dramatized and integrated within administrative security apparatuses whose function is not to wage a battle against an enemy but to regulate mobility within and into the EU. Within a liberal rationality, security is not so much about the staging of an existential threat as about a form of 'targeted governance' (Valverde and Mopas 2004) aimed at groups deemed unqualified for the autonomous exercise of freedom and mobility.

Considering the liberal logic in more detail, this book empirically examines an array of initiatives developed to manage mobility and immigration risk, ranging from remote control, knowledge-based border management and camps to the involvement of private actors in the risk-driven population management. By examining how security practices in the EU constitute the political, this book seeks to account for the apparent paradox that the EU, a liberal regime concerned with the promotion of cross-border mobility, increasing relies on exclusionary and illiberal practices of security.

Abject mobility and the unmaking of security

The paradoxical coexistence of the Union's focus on free movement on the one hand and its increasing reliance upon practices of security on the other can be understood within the context of a liberal governance of freedom, where groups are made amenable to forms of intervention that are increasingly punitive and exclusionary. Although risk management under liberal conditions of governance may seem more benign that the exceptional practices identified with the realist paradigm of national security and war, risk performs an exclusionary function with pernicious political effects. The governance of freedom in the EU introduces a break in life between forms of life that are described as responsible and those that are considered bogus. It fragments populations into different categories which are subjected to different forms of power, regulation and control. Following Rose, risk management is best described as an act of abjection:

> Abjection is an act of force. This force may not be violence, but it entails the recurrent operation of energies that initiate and sustain this casting off or a casting down, this demotion from a mode of existence, this 'becoming abject'. Abjection is a matter of the energies, the practices, the works of division that act upon persons and collectivities such that some ways of being, some forms of existence are cast into a zone of shame, disgrace or debasement, rendered beyond the limits of the liveable, denied the warrant of tolerability, accorded purely a negative value (Rose 1999: 253).

The abjection of immigrants, especially so-called illegal immigrants, in the EU is apparent. Risk technologies such as camps, airport holding zones, visa requirements and expulsion seek to regulate a form of abject mobility. Here, the identification of the liberal self takes place 'through a repudiation which produces a domain of abjection', the '"unliveable" and "uninhabitable"' zones of social life' designed for 'those who do not enjoy the status of the subject' (Butler 2003: 3). The abject, as Aradau (2007: 60) rightly notes, thus only exists as the limit to the domain of subjectivity, i.e. the cast offs of the liberal order. As a consequence, immigrant voices are often not considered as political voices engaged in a struggle. Securitized as illegal immigrants and bogus refugees, their political agency is denied (Aradau 2004).

For example, acts of resistance (hunger strikes, the sewing of lips and eyes, and even suicide) by rejected asylum-seekers are seen as irresponsible choices made by free individuals aimed at manipulating society. Thus former Belgian Interior Minister Patrick Dewael described a hunger strike by 300 Afghans threatened with expulsion as a form of 'blackmail' (The Guardian 2003), while the former Dutch Minister for Integration, Rita Verdonk, complained that the 'media hype' about asylum-seekers' protests against her plan to expel 26,000 undocumented asylum-seekers would merely cause these asylum-seekers 'to believe that they can simply overturn the process by self-mutilation' (cited in Institute of Race Relations 2004).

Equally, undocumented immigrants that cannot be expelled to their country of origin are often detained in exit centres with the aim of 'convincing' them that return is the best way to exercise their freedom. Dorn Andras, director of Bern police, explains the function of exit centres in the management of undocumented immigrants in Switzerland, a signatory of the Schengen agreements, as follows:

> The asylum-seekers we bring up here are ones that should leave Switzerland. By putting them in the (exist centres), they will not feel comfortable and they will realise Switzerland doesn't want them anymore – so they will have to accept the decision and leave ... The accommodation we provide for refugees is already very basic. So for rejected asylum-seekers I had to find something of an even lower standard, and that meant it had to go underground (cited in Fekete 2005).

Furthermore, risk management tends to promote a technical discussion of immigration that suppresses a more fundamental political debate about who should be allowed access to the social fabric of society.

In an attempt to unmake the relations of power that turn immigrants into risky populations, the final aim of this book is to argue in favour of a form of belonging that is not organized around the mediation of risk and fear. Instead of viewing the actions of migrants as dangerous to the EU, the struggle of immigrants could also be regarded as a strategic, political practice that is *constitutive* of community, EU-citizenship and freedom. In particular, Chapter 6 suggests that there is much to gain from thinking of the abject as a political category. Rather than repressing the other as the abject that makes freedom impossible, we should rethink our political community from the standpoint of those that are rendered abject. As Balibar puts it: '[W]e must attack the obsessive question of collective insecurity by beginning precisely with the situation of the most 'insecure', the nomadic populations who are the source of and target of the obsession with law and order that is so closely intertwined with the obsession with identity' (Balibar 2004: 177).

Drawing on the work of Rancière and Balibar and its uptake in security studies, this book points at the possibility of reinventing European belonging from the standpoint of the abject. It does so by considering the struggle in which the *sans-papiers* (undocumented immigrants) movement in France has been involved. While abject populations often remain out of sight, relegated to spaces of exclusion that renders them invisible, recounting their actual struggles against security brings the agency of the abject into vision (Nyers 2003). It bears witness to the reasons for which immigrants risk expulsion and exclusion in their refusal to be governed as abject populations. The struggle of the *sans-papiers* movement exemplifies that universal forms of belonging around the right to free movement depend on the verification, demonstration and re-inscription of that right. They acknowledge that the rights of free movement are simultaneously present (as written inscriptions and in discursive statements on EU-citizenship) and non-present (not enacted). The *aporia* of rights as both present and absent functions as the necessary background condition for forging new forms of belonging (rights are out there to be taken). In the EU, then, political belonging and questions of European citizenship necessarily unfold through arguments, struggles, verifications and denials about the already existing rights of freedom and mobility.

EU-citizenship is not just a status; it is a practice that unfolds in the space between members and outsiders.

The content of this book

This book consists of five chapters. The first three are dedicated to the institutional dynamics of threat construction and examine how immigration has been interpreted as a security issue at the expense of other discourses. In doing so, they trace security discourses and analyze to which degree these are reflected and rooted in treaties, decision-making structures, policies and budgets. Chapter 2 begins by scrutinizing the specific institutional configuration of cooperation in the field of immigration and examines how security professionals working in the area of internal security have managed to frame immigration as a security issue. Because much cooperation in the pre-Maastricht years took place on an informal, even secretive, basis, Chapter 2 makes use of the accounts of actors involved in the decision-making process such as representatives from national ministries (Rupprecht 1989; Rupprecht and Hellenthal 1992; Rupprecht 1993; Nanz 1995), the European Commission (de Lobkowicz 1994; Fortescue 1995; de Lobkowicz 2002; Fortescue 2002), the European Parliament (Esders 1995), security professionals (Wrench 1996), the Schengen/Benelux secretariat (Kruijtbosch 1993; van de Rijt 1998) and NGO representatives (Busch 1989; Bunyan 1991). Besides these accounts, I have also benefited from earlier studies on European police cooperation, especially those undertaken by Bigo (1996) and the Edinburgh school of police studies (Benyon, Turnbull et al. 1993; Benyon, Turnbull et al. 1994; Benyon 1996).

Chapters 3 and 4 focus upon the intergovernmental conferences (IGC) of Maastricht and Amsterdam respectively.[9] These IGCs are conceptualized as institutionalized 'moments of openness' with potentially disrupting effects on the security framing of immigration. Reading these IGCs as political interferences in the bureaucratic procedures and routines, I ask in which ways they have reinforced, reified, uprooted or displaced the interpretation of immigration as a security issue. Despite the commonsensical understanding of immigration as a security issue, the discussion of the Maastricht and Amsterdam IGCs aims to show that there is nothing natural or self-evident about the security nature of immigration.

These chapters also illustrate the liberal logic of security at work. Whereas Maastricht institutionalized the connection between free movement and security, the Amsterdam treaty in particular has given rise to targeted interventions to manage immigration risk. Moving somewhat away from the institutional dynamics of threat construction, Chapter 5 shows that post-Amsterdam security has become a question of targeting risky spaces (airports, third countries), populations (asylum-seekers, undocumented immigrants) and activities (travel, human trafficking) involving an array of interdependent practices such as visa-policy, carrier sanctions, liaison officers, the camp and knowledge-based border management. Finally, Chapter 6 seeks to resist the security frame and calls for the unmaking of security. Whereas the security frame can be resisted on different grounds, this chapter argues that, ultimately, security can only be unmade when we accept that politics is the setting up of a dispute where the abject confront society with a claim to be recognized as equal.

2
Immigration and The Emergence of a European Threat Environment

> Any fact becomes important when it's connected to another. The connection changes the perspective; it leads you to think that every detail of the world, every voice, every word written or spoken has more than its literal meaning, that it tells us of a Secret. The rule is simple: Suspect, only suspect.
>
> Umberto Eco[1]

Introduction

The securitization of immigration should be considered in relation to the emergence and development of a distinct European threat environment and a discussion of how this environment has contributed to the institutionalization of immigration as a security issue. This chapter investigates the ways in which security professionals have produced the meaning of immigration as part of a European 'security continuum' (Bigo 1996) that also includes issues such as terrorism, drugs trafficking, organized crime and human trafficking. In doing so, it will focus predominantly on the bureaucratic level, while the next two chapters will consider in more detail how the bureaucratic level has related to the political level. To focus on the bureaucratic level, however, presupposes that we know these security professionals as well as the threat environment in which they operate. In security studies, researchers have generally focused upon the institutional settings of diplomacy and war to study how key actors such as state leaders, the military, diplomats and foreign affairs officials have defined security at the level of international society (Bull 1977; Der Derian 1987; 1992). Within the context of European threat management, however, the traditional institutional environment only plays a marginal role in the management of the European security continuum. In fact, as the institutional threat environment within Europe is more concerned with societal than military threats, the professional threat environment exists predominantly of actors that work within the field of internal security and public order.

The next section, therefore, will trace the discourses and processes through which these internal security experts have tried to securitize the issue of immigration. It will focus upon Schengen, Trevi, the Ad Hoc Working Group on Immigration (AHWGI) and the Coordinators' Group. Yet, while tracing the processes of securitization in the European threat environment says something about the authority to speak 'security' about immigration, it tells little about how these security platforms have succeeded in providing the hegemonic understanding of immigration in terms of security. Security professionals do not operate in a vacuum but are in constant competition with other professionals that seek to define immigration from the standpoint of alternative ideational backgrounds. The following section, therefore, examines the ways in which security interpretations have closed off and managed to crowd-out alternative enunciations about immigration. It will do so by analyzing the institutional conditions and constraints under which security professionals have put forward their understanding of immigration. Finally, this chapter considers some of the consequences of interpreting immigration and asylum in terms of security. While the security discourses of internal security professionals have owed much of their success to their claim to provide politically neutral solutions, this section shows that the securitization of immigration has in fact had important political, legal and normative consequences for the way in which the EU relates to third country nationals.

Who speaks? Security and the constitution of authority

The question of how the authority to speak security is constituted is generally ignored in European integration accounts of the emergence and development of a European politics of internal security. Here, the development of a European politics of internal security is often historicized as a series of successive moments that have added up to the present state. In this view, past forms of cooperation (Schengen,

Trevi, the Ad Hoc Working Group on Immigration (AHWGI) and the Coordinators' Group) are all viewed as precursors, experimental working sites or laboratories for current constellations (see e.g., Knelangen 2001: 109; Monar 2001: 750). As Klaus-Peter Nanz, Head of the Home Affairs Division of the Permanent Representation of Germany to the EU, argues:

> From the very beginning, the Schengen States have understood the Schengen project as a precursor, a 'laboratory' for free movement of persons in the Union. It is an attempt to combine two seemingly diverging goals: first the abolition of internal border controls for the sake of free movement of persons, with the creation of compensatory measures to strengthen external border controls, and second to fight drug-trafficking, crime and illegal immigration (Nanz 1995: 29).

Dealing with the emergence of a European politics of internal security, the past is often linked to the present in an evolutionary and linear-progressive way, privileging historical constants and continuities over breaks and irruptions. As a consequence, (neofunctionalist-inspired) accounts of the European internal politics of security tend to provide causal accounts along the following lines: At first, borders disappeared, which gave rise to undesirable forms of movement; these forms of movement triggered security measures such as Schengen, which in turn were further developed and formalized in the EU *acquis* on justice and home affairs (see e.g., Knelangen 2001; Monar 2001; Müller 2003; Occhipinti 2003). While this produces parsimonious narratives with a clear beginning and end, the problem of writing the history of current cooperation arrangements in these terms is that it presents the present as unambiguous, singular and perhaps even necessary.

However, while still relatively recent, the history of European internal security cooperation is not one unbroken movement beginning with the signing of Schengen and ending with current cooperation schemes. To the contrary, a closer look at Schengen and the conditions under which it emerged challenges the ways in which present security arrangements recognize themselves in their 'precursors'. For opposite to the assumptions of Nanz and others, compensatory security measures were *not* at the core of the original 1985 Schengen Accord and to present it in this way misses the crucial point that Schengen was concerned more with the abolition of borders than with the potential negative consequences thereof. Schengen, then, was not so much a laboratory for the EU as a competing system for integration, providing an alternative and more speedily road towards free movement. Hence, the original objective of the 1985 Schengen Accord unequivocally speaks of '*removing the obstacles* to free movement at the common frontiers between the States of the Benelux Economic Union, the Federal Republic of Germany and the French Republic' (Schengen Agreement 1985: emphasis added). No mention is made of compensatory measures. In effect, the text of the treaty strongly indicates that such concerns, while present, were not at the core of the agreement. A majority of the 33 articles of the accord concern the facilitation of cross-border transport, while only three articles refer to compensatory measures in the field of internal security and immigration.[2]

Apart from the relatively few textual references to security, the professional backgrounds of the actors that negotiated and concluded the first Schengen agreement also reflect that security was only a minor concern. Preoccupied with the problem of customs controls for cross-border transport, the main actors involved were not, as one would expect on the basis of accounts that invoke Schengen as a 'laboratory' or 'pilot project', internal security professionals but representatives from the Ministries of Transport and the Benelux Secretariat.[3] Indeed, the conclusion of the Schengen Accord was not a response to security concerns but to the 1984 road blockades thrown up by French lorry drivers, who protested against the extensive controls by customs officials, which caused them long delays on their trans-European routes (Wallace 1999: 512). Effectively blocking traffic inside and into France, the strike had significant repercussions for the transport sector in the Benelux countries, France and Germany, which persuaded the governments of these countries of the need to facilitate cross-border transport.[4] This in turn led to the signing of two bilateral agreements – both of which are mentioned in the preamble of the Schengen Accord – in which the abolishment of internal frontiers was regulated: The 31 May Neustadt/Aisch agreement between Germany and the Benelux countries and the 13 July 1984 Saarbrücken agreement between France and Germany.

At the same time, the Benelux Secretariat, which risked becoming administratively redundant as a result of the introduction of free movement on the higher level of all member states, saw in these bilateral agreements an opportunity to extend its original mandate beyond the Benelux. Experienced with coordinating free movement in the Benelux area, the secretariat offered it expertise and helped to bring the bilateral agreements of Neustadt/Aisch and Saarbrücken under the roof of the Schengen Accord (Bigo 1996: 114; Jobard 1999).

To study the securitization of immigration on the European level, therefore, it is not enough to simply replay the dominant historical logic operative in many accounts of internal security. Looking at the conditions of its emergence, it has not been self-evident that Schengen would develop into one of the pillars of current security arrangements. The emergence of Schengen as a crucial platform for security is to be explained rather than taken for granted: What 'happened' that allowed Schengen to develop from a body concerned with free movement to one of the bodies concerned with compensatory security measures? What is needed, therefore, is a perspective that does not stress the continuity but rather the discontinuity and nonlinearity of the emergence and development of a European politics of security. Instead of cultivating the past in terms of the present, the Europeanization of immigration as a security issue should be understood by investigating the conditions of possibility that allowed security professionals to mobilize their discourses and knowledges within particular forums around particular stakes.

Schengen

Although concerns about security were not at the heart of the 1985 Schengen Agreement, a few articles in the treaty text nevertheless referred to internal security concerns. For instance, article 7 states explicitly that:

> The parties shall endeavour to approximate as soon as possible their visa policies in order to avoid any adverse consequences that may result from the easing of controls at the common frontiers in the field of immigration and security. They shall take, if possible by 1 January 1986, the steps necessary with a view, in applying their procedures for the issue of visas and admission to their territory, to taking into account the need to assure the protection of the entire territory of the five States against illegal immigrants and

activities which could jeopardize security (Schengen Agreement 1985: article 7).

Again, this is not to say that the Schengen Agreement therefore constitutes a clearly discernible moment in the development of a European politics of security that also includes immigration. As argued above, the first Schengen Agreement did *not* focus predominantly on security and compensatory measures. Rather, the first Schengen accord is interesting because it is the first official text in which the abolishment of internal frontiers is discursively linked to the need for compensatory measures in the area of internal security and immigration. And although the notion that states were to take 'complementary measures to safeguard security and combat illegal immigration' (Schengen Agreement 1985: article 17) was not of central concern for the actors involved at the time, it is nevertheless important because of the connection it establishes. This connection has provided security professionals with a stake in the management of free movement in Europe and helped change the perspective on immigration. Indeed, since Schengen, the association between free movement and security would become a standard reference in all policy documents on free movement; from then on, it was no longer a question of free movement alone but a question of free movement *and* compensatory measures.

The insertion of the link between free movement and compensatory measures has enabled security professionals working within the national ministries of justice and the interior to gradually 'take over' Schengen. As power also rests on consent, the discursive link between free movement and internal security enabled security professionals to establish their *right* to act and to be involved in issues pertaining to the introduction of free movement, the abolition of borders and the development of the internal market. Strategically exploiting the openings provided by articles 7 and 17 in the 1985 Agreement, therefore, internal security professionals managed to shift the focus of Schengen from the original objective of abolishing borders to one of providing internal security. This shift in focus is also reflected by the fact that the representatives for Transport, responsible for the drafting first Schengen Agreement, were increasingly crowded-out by Justice and Home Affairs representatives in the course of the negotiations on the 1990 Schengen Convention. While the Ministers of the Interior did not conclude the negotiations – a task traditionally reserved for the Foreign Affairs Ministers – internal security representatives played a determinative role in the working groups that were set up to draft the Schengen Convention. More specifically, the negotiations were conducted in four groups: police and security; movement of persons; transport; and customs and the movement of goods (see also Benyon, Turnbull et al. 1993: 135–137) which, as Heiner Busch (1989; 1999) of the German *Institut für Bürgerrechte & öffentliche Sicherheit* has observed, were in turn divided in several subgroups where internal security experts came together to discuss the security implications of the abolition of internal borders. Regardless of whether or not the scenarios of these security experts reflected realistically the consequences of the abolition of internal frontiers (which, in fact, they did not), such statements nevertheless obtained the status of 'truth', as they were uttered within a professional context that added a sense of authority to these security enunciations. As Knelangen argues, it is therefore not important whether the perceived 'security deficit' was real or not:

> What is decisive, rather, is that in the perception of the leading actors from national ministries of Justice and the Interior as well as high-ranking representatives from the police borders are seen as a central element in combating crime. Their disappearance could therefore only be accepted if they would be flanked by compensatory measures of a policing nature. (My translation)

As Wouter van de Rijt (1998), a representative of the Schengen Secretariat, has argued, Schengen permitted working groups to work across various policy domains in order to establish links between them. By moving between the different subgroups, representatives from justice and home affairs were able to connect different issues such as customs, free movement of persons to the issue of internal security. The issue of free movement was no longer to be considered separate from immigration and security, but were now linked together, as security professionals began to explore the links between these hitherto disparate events. For instance, article 96 of the 1990 Schengen Convention refers to the collection of data on 'undesirable aliens' and explicitly connects undocumented immigration to issues of crime, public order and security. The article states that decisions to refuse entry to aliens may be based upon 'a threat to public order or national security and safety which the presence of an alien in national territory may pose', where security is considered to be at stake in the case of (i) 'aliens' that have been previously convicted for a criminal offence, (ii) 'aliens' that have committed a serious offence such a selling of drugs or who have the intention to commit such a crime, and (iii) when the 'alien' has been prohibited entry and who is illegally residing on the territory of one of the member states (Schengen Convention 1990: article 96(2)).

Apart from this article, the increased role of internal security experts in drafting the second Schengen agreement, the so-called 1990 Convention Applying the Schengen Accord, is visible throughout. In fact, the issue of compensatory measures had moved to the very core of the second agreement, where only article 2 concerns the crossing of internal frontiers. All the remaining articles of Title I on the 'abolition of checks at internal borders and movement of persons' deal with the perceived security dimensions of third country immigration such as external border controls (articles 2–8), visas (articles 9–18) and the movement and trafficking of 'aliens' (articles 19–25). In total, only 7 out of 141 articles do not relate to compensatory measures in the area of internal security with 17 articles specifically addressing the cross-border movement of (illegal) immigrants. The convention also foresees in the introduction of the Schengen Information System (SIS) – a database for the purpose of border checks and controls – which is explicitly viewed as a tool in the fight against 'undesirable aliens' (Schengen Convention 1990: Title I).

The qualitative change between the first and second Schengen agreement, then, did not occur because participants in the drafting of the Schengen Accord suddenly 'discovered' a connection between two seemingly divergent facts which until then had remained hidden. The causal relation between the abolishment of borders and an increase in insecurity is much less clear-cut than often assumed. Rather, the change is a direct effect of a change in the professional dispositions of the actors that drafted the first agreement (transport and foreign affairs officials) and the internal security professionals involved in the negotiating and drafting of the second agreement. Meanwhile, the discourse of compensation measures had also been taken up by other institutions (i.e. Trevi, the AHWGI and the Coordinators' Group) with a functional interest in the management of European internal security.

Adopting the compensatory measures discourse, these actors were engaged in a professional struggle with Schengen for the authoritative governance of threats in a borderless Europe.

Trevi

One of the organizations to challenge Schengen was Trevi,[6] which was established at the 1975 European Council in Rome with the original objective of fostering European cooperation in the fight against terrorism through an ongoing exchange of information about terrorist activities. Trevi's organizational structure consisted of three levels: a macro-level consisting of ministerial meetings between the Ministers of Internal Affairs; a meso-level of senior officials who prepared the Ministerial Conferences; and a micro-level consisting of four working groups (Benyon, Turnbull et al. 1994). On the micro-level, the objective of 'Trevi I' (1977) was to facilitate the exchange of information on terrorism (Benyon 1996: 362), while 'Trevi II' (1977) was supposed to deal with the practical and procedural aspects of police cooperation such as the exchange of scientific and technical knowledge. Later, its mandate was extended with issues related the preservation of public order such as football hooliganism.[7] Initially, Trevi's operational value was not that significant. It was not based on any formal convention, lacked a common central secretary or information point and between 1976 and 1985 only six meetings were organized (see also Guyomarch 1997: 133).[8] Yet, Trevi nevertheless succeeded in bringing together senior officials and enabled information to be shared in an informal and professional atmosphere. Peter Wrench, who represented the Police Division of the UK Ministry of the Interior in Trevi, summarizes its socializing function as follows:

> Trevi developed the sort of practical working relationships, mutual understanding and commonality of approach between the Member States' police forces, security services and ministries that is important in its own right, and a prerequisite for making legal instruments work effectively. Trevi ensured that people responsible for leading their countries response to terrorism, for example, knew one another personally, had access to a rapid secure communication system and came together to assess the threat jointly. The operational support that flows from the trust and understanding

these contacts developed – and continue to develop – should not be underestimated (Wrench 1996: 40).

The importance of Trevi, therefore, seems to lie less in the consecration of anti-terrorist policies than in its enabling function as the platform from which internal security officials could explore and exchange various kinds of threat assessments of terrorism (see also Bunyan 1991).

In the early years of Trevi, it is possible to detect first attempts to link immigration to European internal security *via* the question of terrorism and political Islam. Indeed, Rupprecht and Hellenthal (1992: 152), both representatives of the German Ministry of the Interior, explain that one of the themes the working group on terrorism (Trevi I) was the exchange of information on 'undesirable aliens' that were considered a threat to the public order. The fear for Islamic state-supported terrorism (especially by Iran, Libya and Syria) as well as existing links between radical leftwing terrorism and Middle East movements – the Red Army Faction (RAF), for example, obtained funding from groups in the Middle East[9] – became a justification for the policing and surveillance of wider Islamic ethnic minorities and diasporas within Europe (Bunyan 1991: 21). In 1987, the Trevi Ministers finalized the practical methods for 'the exchange of information by member States of TREVI on undesirable foreigners from third countries. This concerns foreigners who present a terrorist threat ... Working Group I will continue to study the means for improving the control of persons and goods from regions where there is a high risk on terrorism' (Trevi/AHWGI 1987).

Yet, the inclusion of immigration as a subject matter to be dealt with under the Trevi umbrella did not take off until the mid-1980s, when cooperation in Trevi started to become more substantial in response to Schengen and the compensatory measures discourse. Especially the Anglo-Saxon states were afraid that the smaller group of Schengen states would monopolize questions of internal security at their expense. Expanding the competences of Trevi, a framework which included all EU member states, provided a viable means to regain some ground on Schengen. Following the Schengen-initiated discourse on compensatory measures, Trevi started to refer explicitly to the 1986 Single European Act to widen its competences.

Trevi's appropriation of the 'compensatory measures' discourse also meant that Trevi became more visible in debates about European internal security and immigration. Whereas Trevi had developed in a relatively anonymous sense as an informal and somewhat secretive platform for law enforcement, it became more public in the mid-1980s, as it tried to position itself as the legitimate guardian of free movement. In 1987, for instance, the Trevi ministers stated in their first public declaration ever that the questions of terrorism, illegal immigration and drug trafficking 'are essential from the perspective of the realisation of free movement within the Community, as the Single European Act provides for' (Trevi/AHWGI 1987). The enhanced visibility of Trevi was also backed up institutionally. The Trevi Ministers agreed to start meeting every 6 months and it was decided that a 'Troika' – a committee of the previous, present and future presidents of the Council of Ministers for Internal Affairs – would act as an executive agency. This structure was again improved during the European Council in Madrid in 1989, when a so-called 'Piatnika' was introduced, i.e. a five member agency consisting of the present, the two previous and the following two presidencies (see also Guyomarch 1997: 132; Knelangen 2001: 129; Occhipinti 2003: 32).

The most significant move, at least from the perspective of the Europeanization of immigration as a security issue, was the creation of the new *ad hoc* working group 'Trevi 92' at the 1988 European Council in Athens. The sole objective of this group was to foster cooperation on the purported security consequences relating to free movement. The name of this *ad hoc* working group refers to the 1992 deadline for the completion of the internal market and, as such, seeks to establish an explicit connection between the community goals of the EU on the one hand and the objectives of Trevi on the other. Thus, the Trevi ministers stated in a public declaration of 1989 that 'the achievement of Community goals is also tied to progress in cooperation among governments in fighting terrorism, international crime, narcotics and illegal trafficking of every sort' (Trevi 1989). The findings of 'Trevi 92' also formed the basis for the 1990 Trevi 'Programme of Action relating to the reinforcement of police co-operation and of the endeavours to combat terrorism or other forms of organised crime'. This document proposed a synthesis of arrangements between police and security services and is Trevi's most outspoken illustration of the intertwining of terrorism, policing, customs, immigration and border control: 'The competent Ministers of the Member States are convinced of the need for new requirements for revised co-operation arrangements following the inauguration of the Single European Act and the necessity to reinforce security at their external frontiers' (Trevi 1990). The problematization of immigration in terms of security was further strengthened by cooperation within the framework of the Ad Hoc Working Group on Immigration (AHWGI) which emerged out of Trevi in 1986.

The AHWGI

The AHWGI developed out of Trevi and was established on 20 October 1986 on initiative of the United Kingdom. The establishment of the AHWGI can be seen within the context of a double struggle. First, the establishment of the AHGWI was a direct reaction to attempts by the Commission to communitarize immigration policies. In its 1985 White Paper on the implementation of the internal market, the Commission maintained the view that the provisions on free movement applied to EU member state nationals and third country nationals alike. Barely a week after the White Paper was adopted, the Commission decided to set up a communication and consultation procedure between member states that required them to exchange information on draft measures relating to the entry, residence and employment of third country nationals and their families. In the communication, the Commission also reserved for itself the right to monitor that these measures did not conflict with community policies (European Commission 1985). However, since the 1986 Single European Act did not specify any community competences in the area of third country immigration, five states (Denmark, France, Germany, The Netherlands and the United Kingdom) contested this decision at the European Court of Justice.[10] With the decision of the European Court of Justice on the factual competences of the Commission in this area still pending, the Ministries of the Interior decided to counter plans of the Commission from the start by launching the AHWGI as an intergovernmental body dealing with immigration on the European level (see Lavenex 2001: 87). Although this to some degree could be seen as a compromise where the member states tried to meet the Commission half-way, the Commission opted for a more socio-economic approach towards third country immigrants whereas the AHWGI in fact sought to curb illegal immigration.

Second, the establishment of AHWGI on the UK's initiative could also be regarded as an attempt by the Anglo-Saxon states to keep some control over European immigration policies. As the United Kingdom did not participate in Schengen, the introduction of the AHWGI can, like Trevi, be viewed as an attempt to extend work on the security consequences of third country immigration to all 12 member states. The fact that the AHWGI's organizational structure duplicated Schengen's structure seems to support this conclusion. As in the Schengen Accord, the Commission was granted the status of observer in the AHWGI. Although this may seem straightforward, the Commission had not been involved in any of the work performed under the umbrella of Trevi (from which the AHWGI emerged). The inclusion of the Commission, therefore, can be seen as an indicator that the AHWGI sought the Union's recognition as the legitimate body to discuss the linkages between immigration, security and free movement. Also, the AHWGI consisted of the same working groups as those operative in the Schengen framework: (i) admission and expulsion; (ii) visas; (iii) false documents; (iv) asylum; (v) external borders; and (vi) refugees (see Rupprecht and Hellenthal 1992: 154).

At the same time, however, many officials that participated within the working groups of Schengen also participated in the mirror groups set up under the AHWGI (Bigo 1996: 164). This led to the paradoxical situation that not only was there competition between the different security platforms but also a degree of overlap, duplication, communication and interaction between actors with the same epistemic worldview (Bigo 1994). Thus, although these platforms had a slightly different background and operated under somewhat different institutional settings and conditions, they also shared the common language of compensatory measures through which they could communicate their threats. In this context immigration increasingly emerged as the common currency with which these professionals could exchange their various security concerns to each other. The AHWGI, too, defined their security concerns in relation to the 1986 Single European Act and the establishment of an internal market. At a 1987 AHWGI meeting in Brussels, it was thus argued that a 'reduction in, and finally the abolition of, controls at the internal borders of the Community must be accompanied by, and depends on, a strengthening of controls at the external borders of the Community' (Trevi/AHWGI 1987). At the same meeting, the ministers responsible for immigration agreed to focus specifically on the fight against illegal immigration. However, the measures proposed at this meeting moved beyond this immediate objective by linking the issue of illegal immigration to crime and asylum.

To begin with the former, the ministers responsible for immigration concluded for instance that the opening of borders should not restrict the 'efficiency of controls from the point of view of the fight against illegal immigration from third countries, drugs and crime' (Trevi/AHWGI 1987). Hence, the AHWGI 'exploited' a certain fuzziness that is at the heart of the term 'illegal immigration'. Whereas according to principles of international law illegal immigration refers to migratory movements that fall outside the legally established criteria of international movement, the AHWGI has contributed to a perception of illegal immigration as a concern with immigrant involvement in certain *illegal activities*. The connection to drugs and crime in turn implied that the AHWGI did not just discuss undocumented movement but also the negative consequences of migratory movements in a broader sense. For instance, the task description of the AHWGI subgroup on visas did not just concern illegal immigration but explicitly set out 'to contribute to better controlling the *problems which result from immigration in general*' (Trevi/AHWGI 1987: emphasis added).

As regards asylum-seekers, the AHWGI outlined the need to distinguish genuine asylum-seekers from so-called *bogus* asylum-seekers. Of course, the distinction between political and non-political refugees is not clear-cut. For instance, economic depressions, environmental catastrophes and rape are not recognized as legitimate grounds to seek asylum even though these are often linked to decisions made in the political systems. Moreover, to put it crudely, in practice it makes little difference whether one starves to death or whether one dies from political persecution. I do not wish here, however, to pursue the tricky question of whether the 1951 Geneva Convention regarding the Status of Refugees should be expanded or applied narrowly (but see Hassner 1998).

Instead, I would like to address the point that the distinction between political refugees and non-political refugees (so-called illegal immigrants) has in practice been decided upon on the basis of whether or not immigrants possess the appropriate documents for entry. Thus, while the AHWGI Ministers authorize the right to seek refuge on humanitarian grounds, they also argue that 'it regularly occurs that the request for political asylum is abused' and that one should 'combat this abuse' by the production of less fraud-sensitive documents, strengthened procedures for examination requests and identity checks before arrival on national territory (Trevi/AHWGI 1987). However, to equate the question of illegality to that of possessing invalid or incomplete documentation ignores, as many humanitarian organizations have pointed out, the fact that genuine asylum-seekers are not always in the possessions of the right papers. To govern illegal immigration through the targeting of fraudulent documents thus risks blurring the distinction between asylum-seekers and illegal immigration.

Being-without-documents, then, is not illegal until it is discursively produced as such. Measures to counter illegal immigration do not just respond to an already defined phenomenon; they create the very parameters of their own application by carving out what is illegal and what is not. In everyday life, for instance, the 'undocumentedness' of immigrants is often unimportant in relation to the functions these people fulfil in society either as workers, spouses, neighbours and so on. The very idea of 'illegality', therefore, is an abstraction imposed upon their daily lives. Concerns with asylum abuse and fraud have led to a process of illegalization whereby undocumented immigrants have been constituted as a threat to the internal market. While *bona fide* asylum-seekers are to be governed through the humanitarian apparatuses, the security experts have claimed the authority to manage undocumented immigrants as *bogus* asylum-seekers that are considered illegitimate, illicit and even criminal. Thus the 1990 Trevi Action Programme on police cooperation, terrorism and organized crime considers 'combating illegal immigration' an essential element in the provision of security:

> With regard to the fight against illegal immigration, co-operation between the relevant departments shall include in particular the exchange of information to assess the scope of the phenomenon: the development of migratory flows, the discovery of clandestine immigration networks, the identification of aliens reported for the purpose of refusal to entry to a member State and of aliens likely to compromise public order, the techniques used in the manufacture of travel documents (Trevi 1990: paragraph 5.1).

The illegalization of undocumentedness, then, has made it possible for undocumented immigration to be identified, categorized and managed as a dangerous population. With undocumentedness or illegality as the defining element of their individuality, improperly documented immigrants are treated in a homogenous fashion even though their motives, life stories and circumstances may vary widely. Thus the AHWGI Ministers announced that 'it is recommended to make provision for areas where asylum-seekers can be received during the first phase of the investigation of their request' as a means of managing the 'manifestly unfounded applications' by separating undocumented immigrants from the ones with proper documents (Trevi/AHWGI 1987). Undocumented immigrants are all classified as a danger that needs to be held at a distance from the community to which they form a threat.

If political refugees and non-political refugees have been lumped together because of the illegalization of undocumentedness, the securitization of asylum-seekers has also progressed through the redefinition of the meaning of 'refugee' as laid down in the 1951 Geneva Convention. This Convention takes the point of departure that in legal terms the recognition of refugee status is declaratory, which means that a person 'does not become a refugee because of recognition but is recognised because he or she is a refugee. The declaratory nature of recognition of refugee status under the UN Convention means that all asylum applicants must be protected as refugees until such time as they are recognised or refused recognition' (Guild and Niessen 1996: 116–117). The discourses found in the internal security groups, however, imply a move from a declaratory to a more constitutive understanding of the meaning of refugee. One of the security practices to bring about this shift is the proposal to separate undocumented immigrants from immigrants with documents already *before* they arrive on EU-territory. Thus, the AHWGI declares that the member states 'will ensure, if they consider it appropriate, in some third countries, at the time of embarkation, a control of travellers' documents' (Trevi/AHWGI 1987). However, as asylum can only be sought upon *arrival*, the proposal to control the travel documents of immigrants already upon *departure* effectively prevents immigrants from claiming their legally guaranteed right of a refuge in EU territory.

A second way in which security practices have challenged the declaratory definition of refugees is through the adoption of the 1990

Dublin Convention.[11] Together with the Schengen working group on asylum, the AHWGI drafted the Dublin Convention (15 June 1990) on the responsibility of states for examining asylum applications. The convention – which is habitually regarded as the backbone of the Union's immigration and asylum policy (Geddes 2000; Monar 2001) – seeks to address the problem of 'refugees in orbit', i.e. the problem that states refuse to review asylum claims, which means that applicants can be forced, especially if returning to the country of destination is not a viable option, to perpetually move from one state to another. As this went against the declaratory notion of refugees, the principle of 'first host country' was introduced, meaning that the first country in which an application for asylum was lodged also had the obligation to deal with the application.

At first sight, the Dublin Convention seemed to be an important extension of this view, as it sought 'to ensure that applicants for asylum are not referred successively from one Member State to another without any of these states acknowledging itself to be competent to examine the application for asylum' (Dublin Convention 1990). However, on closer inspection the Dublin Convention seems designed to keep refugees away rather than to regulate their protection and there is a significant difference between the humanitarian principle of 'first host country' and the Dublin Convention notion of 'country of first asylum'. Instead of establishing a protection of the last resort, the Dublin Convention in fact undermines the ability of asylum-seekers to lodge sequential applications in more than one member state ('asylum-shopping'). That is, the Dublin Convention allows states not to review applications of asylum-seekers that arrived in another country first. Furthermore, as the convention does not prohibit refugees to be sent back to third countries, it quickly became the foundation of a set of readmission agreements between EU member states and third countries. Based on the similar principle of 'country of first asylum', these readmission agreements meant that EU states could send refugees back to third states without reviewing their asylum claims. Ironically, then, the Dublin Convention and the readmission agreements that have followed in its wake, have not stopped the problem of refugees in orbit, but have contributed to the phenomenon by allowing the sequential expulsion of refugees.

The Coordinators' Group

Reacting to and reiterating the discourses of the informal groups on internal security, the European Council decided at its December 1988 summit in Rhodes that the community goals were dependent upon compensatory measures:

> The achievement of the Community's objectives, especially in the area without internal frontiers, is linked to progress in intergovernmental cooperation to combat terrorism, international crime, drug trafficking and trafficking of all kind. This cooperation will be stepped up in order to achieve rapid and concrete results which will enable the Community, for its part, to take the necessary measures to turn Europe into a tangible reality for its citizens (European Council 1988).

At the same time, however, it also argued that progress on the introduction of compensatory measures had been slow as a result of the competition and overlap between the various informal security groups. To reduce the complexity in the field of internal security, the European Council therefore established the Coordinators' Group on the Free Movement of Persons with the task of coordinating the different efforts undertaken in the different groups.

From the outset, the Coordinators' Group made clear that it was not just an extra forum for discussing compensatory measures. Since the Coordinators' Group was responsible for 'coordinating, giving an impetus to and unblocking the whole complex of intergovernmental and Community work in the field of the free movement of persons' (Coordinators' Group 1989), it perceived itself to stand on top of, rather than on equal footing with, the other groups dedicated to the management of internal security problems. This was, of course, not completely the case. As the Coordinators' Group derived its mandate from the European Council, it would be clear that Schengen would be excluded from any official tasks in the management of threats on the EU-level. The Coordinators' Group, therefore, did not just coordinate the different efforts; it was also involved in the struggle and competition between these agencies, where it sought to position itself as the highest legitimate instance for managing the threats identified with the introduction of free movement for all 12 EU member states.

At the 1989 Madrid European Council, the Group presented its conclusions in the so-called Palma document, named after the Group's meeting in Palma de Mallorca (4–6 June 1989). The document strictly followed the compensatory measures discourse found in the other bodies since the mid-1980s. However, the document stands out in one important way, as it assigns specific tasks, foreseen from a strict timetable, to the different security groups (but not Schengen!). According to the Palma document, the most-needed short and long term flanking measures to be taken in the field of asylum and immigration are:

(1) The regulation of admission to community territory
- Establishment of a common list of countries whose citizens are subject to visa requirement;
- Establishment of a common list of persons to be refused entry;
- Harmonisation of the criteria and procedures for granting visas;
- Introduction of a common European visa.

(2) The granting of asylum and refugee status
- Determination of the state responsible for examining the application for asylum and the preparation of a Convention concerning this point;
- Conditions governing the movement of applicants between member states;
- Simplified or priority procedure in the case of unfounded applications;
- Databank for storing information on the places and dates of submission of applications for asylum (which also includes information related to the refusal of visas and forged papers)

(Coordinators' Group 1989).

This had important consequences for the securitization of immigration on the European level: Whereas the issue of immigration had been securitized somewhat indirectly by Trevi and the AHWGI, the Palma document brought together all sorts of groups and issues related to internal security and law enforcement and constituted immigration and asylum as a point on what Didier Bigo (1996) has referred to as the 'European security continuum'. Bringing together various separate initiatives, the Coordinators' Group contributed, to the establishment of a more coherent internal security environment that unambiguously connected the questions of immigration, asylum and visas to questions of security and border control, as is expressed in its call for a Europe-wide database that contains, and hence links, information about asylum-seekers, visas and forged papers.

Hence, the Coordinators' Group contributed significantly to the securitization of immigration and asylum-seeking. It accomplished at the level of all EU member states what Schengen had accomplished for the five member states. Moreover, the Coordinators' Group effectively assigned different tasks to different organizations and, in doing so, took an important step towards the formalization of these hitherto largely informally operating clubs that had functioned largely outside the EU structure. By urging the different security groups to work together on the implementation of compensatory measures under strict deadlines, the Coordinators' Group gave an important impetus to the institutionalization of internal security cooperation as a part of the formal EU integration process (see also Chapter 5).

The leverage of the security frame

Through the competition and exchange of threats between the different forums of Schengen, Trevi, the AHWGI and the Coordinators' Group, the issues of immigration and asylum have been constructed and institutionalized on the European level as a threat specifically relating to the implementation of the internal market. However, the fact that the security discourses of the various security clubs increasingly started to converge around the Union's objective of free movement tells us little about why these discourses have proven so powerful outside the epistemic context of security experts. Why did the European Council in 1988 recognize the link between free movement and compensatory measures in the field of immigration? Why did it not, for instance, adhere to other framings of immigration? Why did it ask the Coordinators' Group to give an impetus to compensatory measures? And why, for instance, did it not ask the Commission, the European Parliament or even the Council of Europe to investigate the political and normative questions related to matters of refugee law and flanking measures? What, in other words, made the security interpretations 'stick'?

To answer these questions it is worth recalling the rhetorical force of securitization. As references to security invoke some sort of pre-political priority ('if we don't act now, it will be too late!'), the invocation of security in policy discourses often works as a rhetorical device through which the legitimacy and political support for political action is legitimized (see also Eriksson 2001).[12] Security is one of the indefinite concepts whose deployment automatically mobilizes support by endowing it with a sense of utmost priority. Things we are afraid of or fear often take on high societal salience in decision-making. Arguably, however, this is valid more for questions of 'national security' and 'survival' than for the somewhat less dramatic question of free movement and European internal security. In fact, when security actors started to define threats to free movement in the mid-1980s, they talked about a somewhat distant risk rather than a concrete existential enemy. Nevertheless, Trevi, the AHWGI and the other platforms have generally performed their tasks under a strong sense of urgency by referring to the quickly approaching deadline of 1992 as the moment where the internal market would be introduced. For instance, Trevi's working group on free movement, 'Trevi 92', carried a strong reference to the 1992 deadline, while the earlier established working groups of Trevi went under the much less imaginative names of 'Trevi I', 'Trevi II' and 'Trevi III'. The sense of priority also permeates the 1989 declaration of the Trevi Ministers:

> We conceive the implementation of the Single European Act as an opportunity to give wider effect beyond national boundaries to an essential personal freedom that already exists within those boundaries, namely the freedom of movement ... At the same time, we note with growing concern the development of organised crime across frontiers ... Crimes such as terrorism, drug trafficking, traffic in human beings, as well as the laundering of profits obtained in these and other criminal activities, are now being planned and organised on a transnational scale, taking advantage of all facilities offered by the development of communications and international travel. Furthermore, these facilities bring about certain risks with respect to public order and internal security. The attraction represented by the freedom and prosperity of our societies is itself becoming a source of profit and exploitation of misery for networks

> of illegal immigration, taking advantage of our wish not to impose over-rigorous controls at frontiers on the vast majority of travellers (Trevi 1989).

The message is clear: If we do not immediately act against the perversions brought about by free movement, a security deficit will emerge that will be exploited by criminals, immigrants and human traffickers. In the worst case, public order, internal security and even the very essential personal freedom we cherish are at peril. A similar sense of urgency is found in the Coordinators' Group Palma document, which stresses the need for a great deal of flanking measures to be taken before free movement can be introduced in a responsible manner. Thus, the Coordinators' Group argues that 'in many instances the measures proposed, for example those regarding provisions on immigration ... are ones which are desirable in their own right, though equally their implementation assumes greater *urgency* and *importance* in the light of the objective of free movement' (Coordinators' Group 1989: emphasis added). In its 1992 report to the European Council in Edinburgh, the Coordinators' Group even went as far as to say that in light of the little progressive achieved in the development flanking measures 'it is clear that it will not be possible to remove internal frontier controls on 1.1.1993' (Coordinators' Group 1992).

The sense of urgency inherent in statements about security calls for deeds rather than words: It stresses the necessary and inescapable need to take quick decisions. As such, security is opposed to the often much slower democratic process, which involves communication and argumentative procedures by means of which various actors provide reasons, justifications and evidence as a way of convincing the audience of the need to take certain decision (Williams 2003: 522).[13] This view is also embodied in the Copenhagen School's notion of securitization as a process that bypasses the normal, democratic rules of the game. In one of the few explicit normative passages in their book, the Copenhagen School thus argues: 'National security should not be idealized. It works to silence opposition and has given power holders many opportunities to exploit "threats" for domestic purposes, to claim a right to handle something with less democratic control and constraint ... Basically, security should be seen as a negative, as a failure to deal with issues as normal politics' (Buzan, Wæver et al. 1998: 29).

The non-democratic character of security politics also finds expression in the semi-secret character of the internal security forums. Admittedly, these organizations did not work completely out of public sight. In 1989 the Trevi Ministers even adopted a declaration 'desiring to present to public opinion the spirit and direction of their work and to open to discussion its basic aspects' (Trevi 1989). But in general public declarations were scarce, while all minutes, agendas, members or decision-making procedures of Trevi were kept confidential. As internal security cooperation took place mainly on an informal basis, Trevi, the AHWGI and the Coordinators' Group were therefore relatively free to take decisions outside democratic and judicial debates that characterize more public ways of decision-making. The result was that actors with possible alternative interpretations of how to approach immigration (e.g., the Commission, the European Parliament, the European Court of Justice or the Council of Europe, the United Nations or even national parliaments) had little opportunity to influence the agenda. As Lord John Tomlinson, MEP for the British Labour Party, commented:

> They started off by justifying these private, secret discussions on the basis that they were dealing with questions of security ... Then they extended it to discussions of drug policy ... By the time they extended their agenda to a third subject, the coordination of immigration policy ... they are managing to equate immigration policy and free movement of people with the same level of imperative secrecy as they are saying is necessary to have for counter-terrorist activities and counter drug activities (cited in Bunyan 1991: 22).

Also the drafting of the legal text of the second Schengen Agreement took place in an institutional environment characterized by a lack of democratic and judicial accountability (Monar 2002; Geddes 2003: 134). Moreover, since Schengen was not part of the EU integration process, the European Parliament was not allowed to participate in the process,[14] with texts generally being forwarded to parliaments only after the end of the negotiations.[15] Thus, while the Dutch parliament objected that the Schengen Agreement was in contradiction to the 1951 Geneva Convention regarding the Status of Refugees (Benyon, Turnbull et al. 1993: 140), it could only accept or reject the text in full.

To some extent, the European Commission has played a more ambiguous role. Immediately after the adoption of the 1985 White Paper, it claimed authority for the regulation of immigration, stressing especially the socio-economic aspects related to the entry, residence and employment of immigration (European Commission 1985). However, after the European Court of Justice decided that the Commission did not have the competences thereto, the European Commission opted for a more pragmatic strategy. It no longer objected to the informal nature of cooperation of immigration but rather tried to use its observant status in Schengen and the AHWGI to make sure that these texts did not clash with Community provisions. Although this may have been the only option short of complete marginalization (Geddes 2000: 72), it also implied that the Commission had to accept, if only tacitly, the securitarian logic that connected free movement to compensatory measures.

'Words spoken, deeds done'. The consequences of securitizing immigration

The way in which security has operated in Europe thus differs somewhat from the dramatic vision of security as being about existential threats to survival. While a sense of urgency and priority was no doubt present in utterances on compensatory measures, it is fair to say that European internal security is somewhat removed from the urgency that surrounds the loaded concepts of 'national security', 'survival' and 'existential threats'. This has not meant, as could be expected, that European politics of internal security has been less speedily and more open to public decision; instead, practices of security have been channelled into informal routines, epistemic communities and networks such as Trevi and the AHWGI, which have operated largely outside public vision. Still, rather than being about distinct speech acts, the securitization of immigration has come about as a result of bureaucratic discourses that have gradually rendered the issues of immigration and asylum susceptible to professional risk calculations and threat assessments related to the introduction of free movement. In a sense, the 'exciting' language of national security has given way to the more bureaucratic language of risk and risk management. In this language, friend and enemy are not considered as two, mutually exclusive groupings, but as end points on a continuum of threats that are governed through calculations about the risk they involve. Hence, risk management does not focus upon existing existential threats, but seeks to intervene before the situation reaches to the point of extremity in which exceptional measures are called for. It is an 'attempt to pre-empt or dedramatize conflict by acting upon the physical and social structures within which individuals conduct themselves' (Rose 1999: 237). The everyday processes of securitization visible in Trevi or the AHWGI thus recode and re-inscribe the dramatic play of survival and existential threats into a more technological and diffuse management of events and processes that are identified as threats to free movement and the internal market (see also Chapters 3 and 4).

The technocratic and somewhat routine-like character has been an important factor for the success of the security frame. For while a speech act that invokes 'extraordinary measures' that bypass legal and political constraints is likely to invoke discussions about civil rights and liberties as well as community obligations towards outsiders, the informal platforms have largely managed to circumvent these discussions due to the technocratic nature of their discourses. As Guiraudon summarizes: 'The technical appearance of the texts on the one hand promotes the impression of the existence of "easy" solutions to a complex problem and, on the other, expresses a limited ambition in these measures, since the treaties do not touch substantive matters of refugee law but indicate that they are to be restricted to the measures necessary in fulfilling the goal of European integration' (Guiraudon 2001: 101). Questions concerning how the politically sensitive issues such as immigrant rights and humanitarian obligations should be dealt with on the European level were carefully avoided. Thus the Coordinators' Group argued that 'the (Palma) report in general and the recommendations for measures to be taken, represent practical steps upon which all could agree and do not prejudice the legal and political questions' (Coordinators' Group 1989). It was thus difficult for other actors, especially for the pro-integration ones, to argue against these discourses. For instance, the European Parliament stressed on several occasions that states should retain a liberal asylum policy according to the international principles of humanitarian law (European Parliament 1987), but on no occasion are humanitarian concerns addressed in relation to compensatory measures and free movement.[16]

Thus although risk management appears as a somewhat technical matter free from normative connotations, it is not neutral to say that immigration is a security problem. As Huysmans argues: 'Migrants are never purely a machine or a number in a calculus. They are captured in a game of domination and subordination and a symbolic game of defining the good and right life' (Huysmans 2000b: 151). To define immigration as a point on the European security continuum logically implies that one designs measures to keep this threat at a distance. Successful or not, compensatory measures such as the increase in border control and identity checks have the purpose to make it difficult for immigrants to enter the European space. Security, therefore, is not just about deciding on the enemy through a passage to the exception; it is also about distributing trust and fear. While the documents and texts of groups such as Schengen and Trevi do not resort to existential threats and the drama of survival, they nevertheless have significant effects through their ability to define the groups that are to be feared. As the Chief Inspector of the Copenhagen Police, responsible for the training and education of border guards at Copenhagen airport, explains:

> [Risk] profiling has something to do with spotting persons whose appearance or behaviour is distinct from the others. Those are the ones we focus on and those are the ones we control extra. If you can see that longer down the line there is an Asian person with a Danish-looking passport, you ask yourself: 'Why does he have that?' He would be one of those you single out for control. Perhaps he is a Danish citizen, but you cannot directly see this as such. He has to suffer the burden that every time he ... arrives he will undergo extra control ... so we can make sure that he is a Danish citizen, a Schengen-citizen and don't let him in on a false basis. If we don't do that and just let [him] slip through, then the Dane who is standing behind him will say 'Hey, why is he not controlled?' There is also a psychological element in control (Interview, 24 November 2004).[17]

Border control based upon appearance rather than criminal behaviour thus plays an important role in assuring individuals that everything is under control. However, it also increases the distance between self and other insofar as the image of the other as a suspect is sustained by risk categories that work upon a specific (securitized and racialized) understanding of what is Danish and what is non-Danish or non-Schengen.

When uttered in a bureaucratic context, therefore, security is less about extraordinary measures and questions of life and death than about administrating and governing exclusion. While there are many ways to manage inclusion and exclusion in modern societies (the welfare state being one prominent example), security is a particularly 'violent' form of managing exclusion insofar as it radicalizes the gap between the threatened community and the dangerous outside world (Huysmans 1995). For instance, one can be excluded from the labour market or other social arrangements, but in these cases one is still considered as a legitimate participant in social relations that together make up society. For security to work, however, the other must be portrayed as a threat or a risk to the community, which in turn denies the existence of a common ground for symbolic exchange between the endangered community and the threat. Portrayed as neutral interventions necessary for the process of European integration to continue, the securitization of immigration has a broader impact upon the political and normative questions of how to treat outsiders.

On top of that, the security logic risks becoming self-propelling in the sense that measures aimed to increase security in fact may trigger more insecurity. As the conventional ways of entering EU territory are proving increasingly unattractive to immigrants that want to move to the EU, it has been argued that refugees without appropriate documents are left little alternative than to turn to organized forms of trafficking and smuggling (e.g., Guild and Niessen 1996: 118; Andreas 2000; Guiraudon 2001). However, their reliance upon human traffickers also adds to the view that they are economic immigrants that merely want to enter the EU illegally, which in turn supports the call for new and more sophisticated security responses. Although designed to bring illegal immigration and organized trafficking to a halt, policing practices may well create the very conditions to which they claim to provide a solution. Attempts to increase controls and reinforce the distance between third country immigrants and the host community thus automatically also produce more danger. The production of security, therefore, is simultaneously also the production of *in*security. Security 'does not radically cut off the subject from what threatens it – on the contrary, abjection acknowledges it to be in permanent danger'

(Kristeva 1982: 10). Or as Ole Wæver has argued, security, the force of abjection, can never provide a way out of the security dilemma:

> *[S]ecurity* and *insecurity* do not constitute a binary opposition. 'Security' signifies a situation marked by the presence of a security problem *and* some measure taken in response. Insecurity is a situation with a security problem and *no* response. Both conditions share the security problematique. When there is no security problem, we do not conceptualize our situation in terms of security; instead, security is simply an irrelevant concern. The statement, then, that security is always relative, and one never lives in complete security, has the additional meaning that, if one has such complete security, one does not label it 'security'. It therefore never appears. Consequently, transcending a security problem by politicizing it cannot happen *through* thematization in security terms, only *away* from such terms (Wæver 1995: 56, emphasis in original).

More security, in this view, also implies the further estrangement between third country immigrants and the community deemed at risk. Although security seeks to reassure the public through the management of danger and fear (embodied in the figure of the immigrant) the security solution to the security dilemma does not solve insecurities but contributes to their continued existence by disavowing the existence of a common ground for communication between the 'endangered' community and third country nationals. The distancing logic that underpins security manifests itself very concretely in the practice of border control and other measures of risk management.

These practices may appear to provide practical solutions free from any of the political, legal and normative disputes surrounding the question of immigration, but the politicization of immigration in terms of security actually has an important impact on these questions. If security measures cannot thwart the insecurity spiral, then security may not just radicalize the distance to immigrants; it also creates the very security problems it seeks to solve.

Conclusion

As Umberto Eco's epigraph to this chapter suggests, the connection between immigration and security is not as natural and self-evident as presented in some accounts on the emergence of a European politics of internal security. Moreover, the connection has changed the perspective on immigration. In this chapter, the change of perspective has been claimed to be the instance of internal security experts, who have linked questions of immigration and asylum to the introduction of the internal market and free movement. The origins of the connection between security and free movement can be traced back to the 1985 Schengen Agreement, where it appeared first, if only marginally. Nevertheless, the connection was a relevant one as it enabled security professionals to reconfigure their mandates and discourses around the question of free movement. For instance, for security professionals working together within the Trevi framework the discourse of free movement enabled them to deal with the issue of immigration more directly than they had done in the first decade of their existence. After the European integration process had come to a halt in the 1970s, integration gained new momentum in the mid-1980s through the idea of a people's Europe, which made the development of a European citizenship dependent upon the removal of internal barriers. Although in the 1980s and 1990s the process of European integration was viewed as key to the development of an economic prosperous and geopolitical stable Europe, the integration process was paradoxically also deemed to undermine European internal security (and hence prosperity and stability!).

This typically European discourse has also paved the way for the securitization of immigrants *via* the question of illegality and asylum-seeking. On the one hand, the notion of illegal immigration allowed for linkages to be made between immigrants, illegal movement and illegal activity; on the other hand, concerns with immigrants abusing the asylum system led to general measures of law enforcement directed at all potential asylum applicants. At the same time, the intergovernmental and secretive nature as well as the sense of urgency and priority related to many of the security provisions in the field of immigration and asylum policies ensured that alternative actors such as the Commission, the European Parliament, pro-migrant NGOs, the European Court of Justice and national parliaments were unable to put their stamp on these policies.

The technological character of the security discourses, moreover, gave the impression that the problem of immigration could be solved through measures of control without compromising legal, political and normative questions surrounding immigration and one's self-understanding in liberal and humanitarian terms. Yet, the authority of security professionals to govern immigration has had significant implications on the relations between the EU and third country nationals. As Andrew Geddes has noted, 'EU level chances for migrant inclusion are structured by the institutional context and the conceptualisations of the migration *problematique* that underpins it' (Geddes 2000: 4). But if the governance of immigration since the mid-1980s was first and foremost embedded within the institutional context of law enforcement, the 1990s witnessed an increasing communitarization of asylum and immigration policies. Whether this also has led to a less security-oriented view where other institutional actors have been able to claim the authority to govern and manage immigration is the topic of the next two chapters.

3
The Maastricht Treaty: The Formalization of the Immigration/Security Nexus

Introduction

So far, this story has stressed the significance of the enunciations of security professionals for the creation of immigration as a security problem. In this chapter, I consider in which ways the 1992 Maastricht Treaty has impacted upon the representation of immigration as part of a European security continuum that also includes terrorism, organized crime and drug trafficking. The purpose of this chapter, therefore, is to provide an overview of the institutional outcomes of the Maastricht Treaty and to analyze the consequences thereof for the scope and limits of the European internal security field: How have political negotiations involving member states and high level bureaucrats such as the European Commission modified, changed, reified, reshuffled or transformed the symbolic positions from which actors can successfully speak 'immigration'? And to what extent has the Treaty of Maastricht allowed or constrained security professionals to define the 'truth' about immigration within the institutional context of the European Union? As such, the aim of this chapter is not so much to provide a detailed account and analysis of the negotiations leading up to the signing of the Maastricht Treaty.[1] Rather, it intends (i) to examine in which ways (if any) the Maastricht Treaty has embedded security statements about immigration and asylum into the official working structures and policies of the EU and (ii) to analyze what effects this has had upon the securitization of immigration on the European level.

In the previous chapter the authoritative capacity to define European threats was first and foremost located at the *bureaucratic* level of security professionals working together in Schengen, Trevi, the AHWGI and the Coordinators' Group. By considering the *political* level of intergovernmental negotiations, this chapter slightly shifts the focus of the narrative. The reason for doing so is that intergovernmental conferences can be viewed as structured moments of dislocation with the potential to undermine, transform or strengthen existing security discourses on immigration. On the one hand, the formalization of security platforms can consolidate or even strengthen the position of the pre-Maastricht security clubs insofar as the inclusion of these clubs into the official structure is likely to add a sense of political legitimacy to their enunciations. On the other hand, their position may also be weakened as the inclusion of these clubs in the formal cooperation structures increases their public visibility, which may subject security enunciations to alternative validity claims about immigration. In fact, intergovernmental conferences may even relocate the authority to enunciate 'immigration' to professional contexts that are not concerned with threat management at all. Thus, although the political level is not the most crucial one in defining what constitutes a threat, the way security discourses are (or are not) embedded institutionally cannot be accounted for without a discussion of the intergovernmental negotiations and their institutional outcomes.

Hence, this chapter examines the ways in which the intergovernmental conference leading up to the Maastricht Treaty helped to make intelligible a particular 'regime of truth' about immigration. To this end, the next section reviews the member state negotiations and considers the ways in which these have allocated the symbolic authority to speak 'immigration'. It will be argued that the member state negotiations have largely incorporated the already existing informal security groups within the so-called JHA pillar of the newly erected European Union. To discuss in more detail what this has implied for the different actors' capacity to successfully define the issues of immigration and asylum, the following sections will examine, first, the working structures of the JHA pillar and, second, the capability of supranational actors to frame the immigration issue after the introduction of the JHA pillar.

Member state negotiations: Allocating symbolic authority

The idea to organize an IGC emerged after the entry into force of the Single European Act in July 1987, when the 1989 Strasbourg European

Council decided that an IGC should be held to work out the practical details of launching an economic and monetary union (European Council 1989). In the early 1990s, however, several member states proposed that the agenda of the coming IGC should be extended to include political issues (France/Germany 1990a),[2] which was officially adopted by the Dublin European Council in 1990 (European Council 1990). Although originally the notion of a political union was related to the wish to enhance the democratic character of decision-making and the desire to increase the external profile of Europe in light of the Gulf War, the conflict in former Yugoslavia, German reunification and the end of superpower overlay in Europe, the question of internal security emerged on the political agenda after a joint Franco-German statement on 6 December 1990. In this letter, addressed to the Italian Prime Minister Andreotti, in his capacity as President-In-Office of the European Council, the French President François Mitterrand and the German Chancellor Helmut Kohl argued:

> We would like the intergovernmental conference to define the bases and structures of a political union that features strength and solidarity, is close to the citizen and committed to the direction laid out by its federal nature. As regards the competences of the union and the Community, we propose that they be deepened and enlarged ... Certain issues that are currently handled in an intergovernmental context could enter the scope of the union: immigration, visa policy, right of asylum, anti-drug actions, measures to fight international organized crime. Consideration could be given to setting up a Council of Interior and Justice Ministers (France/Germany 1990b).

In terms of its contents, there is little surprising about the joint Franco-German statement. The assumption that immigration should be governed in a similar sense as organized crime, terrorism and drug trafficking had already been forcefully argued in Schengen and other groups claiming that the abolition of borders would require compensatory flanking measures. What is interesting, though, about this statement and its positive reception at the European Council in Rome on 14–15 December 1990 is that the question of internal security management is explicitly linked to the more general question of institutional design and the establishment of a Council of Interior and Justice Ministers.

The linkage between internal security and the question of institutional design has potentially far-reaching consequences for the securitization of immigration. First of all, the proposal to formalize internal security cooperation can be said to bring issues back to the level where they can be dealt with according to the rules of normal politics rather than those of urgency and priority that had allowed security professionals to operate somewhat outside public scrutiny. Formalization does not resolve securitized issues, but gives them a permanent position in society where they are dealt with in less dramatic ways (see also de Wilde 2005). Second, linking the question of internal security to the question of institutional design may contribute to the undoing of the security frame by transforming the constellation of actors with the authority to define the problems of security and immigration. For although the Franco-German statement did not discursively decouple immigration from the environment of threat management, the mere fact that internal security would be integrated within the wider context and decision-making structures of the European Union implied that the *status quo* of informal groups discussing immigration in a secretive environment would be difficult to maintain completely.

Hence, when in 1991 the Presidency of Luxembourg initiated the intergovernmental negotiations on a political union, the question about cooperation in justice and home affairs immediately evolved into a question of whether or not community institutions such as the European Commission and the European Parliament should be given more competences in the area of internal security. To map the preferences of the member states on this issue, the Council Presidency put forward four possible scenarios in January 1991. The first option emphasized the *status quo* situation of *ad hoc* cooperation in intergovernmental clubs that dominated cooperation on internal security during the 1980s. The second alternative also opted for the continuation of the existing frameworks, but arranged for the Maastricht Treaty to include a general reference to cooperation on internal security. Although this would formalize the connection between the political community objectives on the one hand and the need for cooperation in the field of justice and home affairs on the other, it would leave the practical details and implementation of such cooperation to be worked out on an intergovernmental basis by the European Council. The third institutional set-up envisaged the integration of justice and home affairs within the Treaty with the important qualification that the inclusion of provisions relating to internal security in the community structure would not involve the transferral of member state competences to the supranational level. The last and most far-reaching option foresaw in the full communitarization of cooperation on justice and home affairs (Corbett 1993: 48). Not surprisingly, the preferences of the member states were divided. Denmark opted for the *status quo*, but was generally also willing to accept the second option. Greece, Ireland and the United Kingdom also favoured the second option, whereas the members of Schengen (Belgium, France, Germany and the Netherlands) and its associated states (Italy, Portugal and Spain) were willing to accept a more far-reaching role of the community institutions with Belgium, Ireland, the Netherlands and Spain particularly being in favour of the fourth option.[3] In sum, a clear majority of the member states favoured a partial communitarization of justice and home affairs cooperation somewhere between option three and four. Nevertheless, a revision of the constitutional treaty required unanimity, which implied that a far-reaching communitarization of cooperation on justice and home affairs was unattainable even if it was the preferred option of most member states.

The need for a compromise between the conflicting preferences was reflected in the non-paper produced by the Luxembourg government on 12 April 1991 which proposed an institutional design that was firmly rooted in the *status quo*, albeit with some qualifications. The proposal foresaw in the creation of a union existing of three pillars (an economic and monetary pillar, a pillar for a common foreign and security policy, and a justice and home affairs pillar), each with their own working structure and decision-making procedures. Although the Presidency finally managed to forge an agreement in June 1991, significant controversies still remained. For instance, Germany had not given up its hopes for a communitarized immigration and asylum policy as a means of sharing the responsibility for the inflow of asylum-seekers into Europe. However, states with significantly less asylum-seekers than Germany were not very enthusiastic about the German proposals and continued to resist the idea of 'burden sharing' (Geddes 2000: 90).

Most significantly, perhaps, the Dutch Presidency – who had taken over from Luxembourg in July 1991 – openly advocated the integrative priorities of its own government. It abandoned the Luxembourg compromise of a pillared structure and proposed a tree-like structure of the political union instead. Here, JHA would not be a separate part of the union subject to a high degree of intergovernmental decision-making, but one of the branches of a political union characterized by supranational decision-making. Obvious to everyone but the Dutch Presidency, it was clear that other states would not support such a far-reaching structural reform.[4] Faced with the unwillingness of other states to negotiate justice and home affairs on their terms, the Dutch had no other option but to recognize their diplomatic defeat and return to the original Luxembourg proposals of a pillared structure.

The introduction of a separate pillar of JHA provided an agreeable, if not parsimonious, compromise to all member states. For those unwilling to communitarize policies relating to justice, policing and the control on the entry of non-nationals on national territory, the JHA pillar remained highly intergovernmental with only limited influence for supranational actors. Besides, the preservation of the unanimity rule for decision-making under the JHA pillar meant that hesitant countries would keep the right to veto policy initiatives put forward by the Commission or other member states. In the meantime, the pillar structure was also an agreeable alternative for countries that sought a partial or complete communitarization of justice and home affairs. For them, the JHA pillar represented at least a first step on the road towards more European integration.[5]

On the discursive level few things changed and the third pillar, Title VI on Justice and Home Affairs (JHA), replayed the familiar logic of compensatory measures uttered in the pre-Maastricht contexts of Schengen, Trevi, the AHWGI and the Coordinators' Group. The opening article of the JHA pillar thus explicitly states that, with the aim of achieving the objective of free movement,

> Member states shall regard the following areas as matters of common interest: asylum policy; rules governing the crossing by persons of the external borders of the Member States and the exercise of controls thereon; immigration policy and policy regarding nationals of third country: conditions of entry and movement, conditions of residence, and combating unauthorised immigration; combating drug addiction; combating fraud on an international scale; judicial cooperation in civil matters; judicial cooperation in criminal matters; customs cooperation; police cooperation for the purpose of preventing and combating terrorism,

unlawful drug trafficking and other serious forms of international crime (European Union 1992: article K.1).

Although the Maastricht Treaty thus seemed to continue the pre-Maastricht security rhetoric, the integration of the area of internal security within the wider context and decision-making structures of the European Union also introduced some contingencies and uncertainties as to which actor would be best located to enunciate immigration. The Maastricht Treaty did not specify in significant detail the working structures of the JHA pillar, which – at least in principle – gave the permanent representation to the Council (Coreper) and supranational actors such as the Commission the opportunity to exercise some influence on the management and governance of immigration within the framework of the Union.

The institutional endurance of informal security groups

In terms of the specification of working structures, the Maastricht Treaty only called for the establishment of a coordinating committee in article K.4 TEU. This left open the possibility for the EU to create wholly new working structures that needed not be based on the informal forms of cooperation that already existed parallel to the institutional structure of the Union. In practice, however, the continuity of the free movement/compensatory measures discourse was followed by institutional continuity. The Coordinators' Group, Trevi and the AHWGI were all integrated into the new working structure of the JHA pillar of the European Union. According to Wenceslas de Lobkowicz, a former Commission official in the area of JHA, the institutional continuity can be accounted for by the fact that, after the ratification of Maastricht on 1 November 1993, the Belgian Presidency only had six weeks to fill in the working structures of JHA cooperation (de Lobkowicz 2002: 55). This short time span, he argues, simply did not allow for experimenting with alternative organizational structures.

But it was not just a question of time that made the political leaders decide to build upon the informal structures. It was also a result of the Coordinators' Group's success to position itself as a central player in working out the future working structures. After having accepted the Palma document at the European Council in Madrid in 1989, the 1991 European Council in Maastricht asked the Coordinators' Group to submit a report on the shape of the third pillar working structures. Basically, this mandate gave the Coordinators' Group the possibility to institutionalize more fully the measures it proposed in its Palma document. Hence, in a confidential report to the 1992 European Council in Edinburgh (obtained by the civil liberties NGO Statewatch), the Coordinators' Group put forward its conclusions on the JHA working structures (Coordinators' Group 1992), concluding that the work performed under the aegis of the K.4 Committee should be divided into three areas: (i) immigration and asylum; (ii) security and law enforcement including police and customs cooperation; and (iii) judicial cooperation. Moreover, it concluded that each area should be headed by a Steering Group and suggested that the position of the first two Steering Groups should be given to the AHWGI and Trevi respectively. Moreover, while the Coordinators' Group did not directly put itself forward as a candidate for the future K.4 Committee, its former position as the coordinating body for the AHWGI and Trevi almost automatically implied that this would be the only logical solution. Or as the Coordinators' Group cautiously anticipated its future role: 'Important work will be required beyond 1 January 1993 on the implementation of the Palma programme. The Coordinators' Group believe that there will continue to be a need for them both to co-ordinate that work and to provide a source of advice to the European Council on Title VI matters until the establishment of the K.4 Committee' (Coordinators' Group 1992: Title III, paragraph 9). In short, the working structure of the JHA pillar consisted of a pyramid-like structure of five levels: (i) the Council of Ministers of Justice and Home Affairs; (ii) the Committee of Permanent Representatives (Coreper); (iii) the Committee of Senior Officials (the so-called K.4 Committee); (iv) the three steering groups; and (v) the various working groups set up under these steering groups (see Figure 3.1).

The working structure of the JHA pillar thus differed significantly from the habitual Community working structure, which consists of three levels only (Council, Coreper, working groups). But while the additional levels of the K.4 Committee and the three steering groups represented important legal and organizational innovations in the institutional architecture of the European Union, they also represented a high degree of continuity insofar as the K.4 Committee,

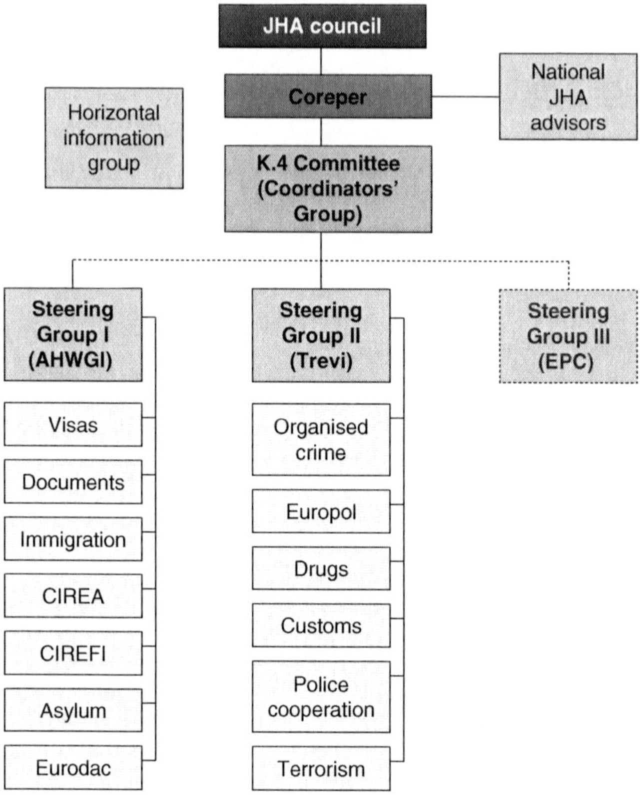

Figure 3.1 Post-Maastricht working structures in the area of JHA
Source: Adapted from Niemeier (1995) and Bigo (1996)

as well as the three steering groups, were based upon pre-existing intergovernmental forms of cooperation on European internal security. The K.4 Committee was composed of the old Coordinators' Group,[6] while the three steering groups were made up of the former AHWGI (now Steering Group I on Asylum and Immigration) and the former Trevi group (now Steering Group II on law enforcement and police and customs cooperation).[7] As Figure 3.1 shows, the K.4 Committee takes a central place in the JHA working structure as the coordinator for the Steering Groups, where all important policy initiatives are developed. At the same time, the K.4 Committee also plays a major role upwards as the body responsible for the preparation of the Council meetings. It also maintains the right to give opinions to the Council on substantial matters relating to internal security, either on the Council's request or on its own initiative.[8] Taken together, this gives the K.4 Committee a considerable leverage over the political agenda-setting phase.

Although the informally operating security platforms managed to secure key position in the new policy-making structures, the internal security officials no longer had direct access to the ministerial level, as has been the case in the pre-Maastricht era. Instead, the K.4 Committee has to report to the Permanent Representation (Coreper), which in turn possessed the sole prerogative to report directly to the JHA Council. The presence of Coreper within the JHA pillar was secured through a reference to article 151 in article K.4.1 of Title VI of the Maastricht Treaty, which stipulates that the K.4 Committee shall 'contribute, without prejudice to article 151 of the Treaty establishing the European Community, to the preparation of the Council's discussions in the areas referred to in Article K.1' (European Union 1992: article K.4.1). According to article 151: 'A committee consisting of the Permanent Representatives of the Member States shall be responsible for preparing the work of the Council and for carrying out the tasks assigned to it by the Council' (European Union 1992: article 151). While some have argued that there exists a clear division of authority between the two bodies (Heukels and de Zwaan 1994: 213–214; Niemeier 1995), others have instead argued that the division of competences between the two levels has 'generated a new series of turf battles in the Council's infrastructure' (Lewis 2000: 275). Indeed, with its traditional focus on Community policies and policy outcomes, Coreper appeared as an odd bedfellow for decision-making in the JHA pillar, where all security expertise was located at the level of the K.4 Committee and the three Steering Groups. Unwilling to share any of its competences with Coreper, the K.4 Committee has even tried to bypass Coreper by directly forwarding texts to the ministerial level (Monar 2002: 196). As Adrian Fortescue, former Head of the JHA Task Force and Directorate-General JHA of Commission as well as a participant–observant in the K.4 Committee has argued, efficient decision-making in the Committee was seriously compromised by the latter's unwillingness to change their pre-Maastricht way of decision-making: '[I]nterior ministers, as their name suggests, were probably always going to be among the least enthusiastic about agreeing to have their habits changed by external pressures coming from the Union' (Fortescue 1995: 26, 27). The differences between Coreper and the K.4 Committee do not just reflect disparities in the way *decisions* are shaped, but also reveal a difference in the way *problems* are shaped or constructed. Because Coreper is involved in EU decision-making processes across different policy-arenas with a responsibility to 'make the system work', its bureaucratic worldview has been less parochial than that of the K.4 Committee, which mediates events, processes and developments in the world through the lens of security (Lewis 1998; 2000; Bostock 2002).

However, if Coreper may to some degree have broken the justice and home affairs monopoly to authoritatively enunciate threats, it also had to make some concessions to both accommodate the concerns of justice and home affairs officials and to compensate for its lack of expertise in the area. To this end, Coreper attached a group of special 'Justice and Home Affairs Advisors' to the permanent representation in 1994 (see also Figure 3.1). This body, made up entirely of national representatives of the ministries of justice and the interior, continued to guarantee a strong presence of justice and home affairs officials on the sub-ministerial level and contributed to the streamlining of policy-making on the five levels.

In sum, then, the internal security representatives working within the context of the AHWGI, Trevi and the Coordinators' Group have been successful in formalizing and consolidating their security interpretations within the institutional structure of the European Union. They managed to secure key position in the new policy-making structures, which guaranteed their continuing existence as a major player in the area of European internal security. Although Coreper has been added as an extra level compared to pre-Maastricht decision-making procedures, it seems fair to say that the authority to enunciate immigration is still firmly rooted in the internal security environment. Wenceslas de Lobkowicz, a former Commission official in the area of JHA, has referred to the particular ability of these groups to secure their own institutional survival, as the 'Trevi blues': 'Ce que d'aucuns appelèrent le 'TREVI *blues*' va se traduire par la volonté de survie, c'est-à-dire par la création des trois 'groupes directeurs': pour l'asile et l'immigration d'abord, pour la coopération policière et douanière ensuite, et enfin pour la coopération judiciaire' (de Lobkowicz 2002: 57). The work performed under Steering Group I (the former AHWGI) continued to work on measures related to the restriction of immigration flows while proposing little in terms of migrant inclusion. To the contrary, the inclusion of all security 'problems' under one institutional structure merely enabled further connections to be made between immigration and various other issues relating to internal security.

This was further reinforced by the creation of the Horizontal Information Group (HIG), CIREA (Centre for Information, Reflection and Exchange on Asylum Matters) and CIREFI (Centre for Information, Reflection and Exchange on the Crossing of Borders and Immigration). Based upon the Schengen Information System (SIS), the HIG enabled connections to be established across the three Steering Groups through the linking of data on immigrants to the databases of organizations dealing with law enforcement such as the Customs Information Database (CIS) and the Trevi database on organized crime. The stated objective of CIREA and CIREFI is to facilitate the exchange of information on migration flows with the aim of improving the governance of immigrants into the EU.[9] While not a speech act in the Copenhagen School sense of the term, the HIG, CIREA and CIREFI have contributed significantly to the securitization of migration through electronic interpellations by means of which certain subjects have become constituted as dangerous or risky.[10] The governance of migration, it is argued, requires knowledge of migration. However, the type of knowledge gathered also determines the kinds of policy measures that are taken. Through the filtering, structuring and categorizing of information on immigration flows, these clearing houses helped to constitute the practical knowledge that make it possible for immigration to be defined and governed through security measures such as visa-regulations, border controls and identity checks.

The institutionalization of informal security clubs implies that in the post-Maastricht era immigration is dealt with on a structural basis without recourse to the dramatic play of priority and urgency that allowed these actors to perform their work outside the normal procedures in the pre-Maastricht period. But while the Copenhagen School equates the process of normalization with that of desecuritization, the normalization and dedramatization of security has not entailed a desecuritization of immigration. Actually, the institutionalization of internal security as part of the EU may well have reinforced the effects of securitization described in the previous chapter. Especially the establishment of HIG as well as the introduction of working groups on CIREA and CIREFI nicely illustrate the way in which the yearning for security can spiral more insecurity: The securitization of illegal immigration inspires the search for more knowledge and information about risks (e.g., immigration flows), which leads to new protection measures (e.g., intensified border controls), which in turn create new insecurities (e.g., human trafficking as a means to circumvent controls), which create the need for more knowledge about these insecurities (e.g., information about the routes used by human traffickers) – and so on.

Furthermore, the formal institutionalization entailed no significant dislocation in the meaning attached to immigration. Rather, it has provided security experts with a common structure or framework within which to interpret and connect problems related to cross border movements in a routinely fashion. The securitization of immigration in the EU is not a question of exceptional measures; rather, it is driven and sustained by the inexhaustible search for detailed and continuous risk management knowledge by security professionals that are predisposed to interpret problems as dangers. Indeed, as the central political debates have centred on the question of competences rather than the prior question of whether the issue of immigration should be dealt with as a security issue in the first place, no attempts have been made to disentangle immigration from internal security. For instance, no proposals were made to deal with immigration as an economic issue (the first pillar) or an issue of foreign affairs (the second pillar). If anything, then, the formal consolidation of a connection between the political objectives of the EU and internal security in the Maastricht Treaty has provided a sense of legitimacy to the bureaucratic context of threat management. As argued by Wenceslas de Lobkowicz, the Maastricht Treaty moved immigration and asylum issues 'out of their *semi-clandestine* institutional set-up and integrated them it into the single institutional structure of the European Union' (de Lobkowicz 1994: 99, emphasis in original). But if the normalization of the informal security clubs has not contributed to a process of desecuritization within the Council working structure, has the formalization contributed to desecuritization by subjecting the enunciations of security experts to the public scrutiny of supranational actors such as the European Parliament, the European Court of Justice and the European Commission?

Supranational actors and the JHA pillar

The constellation of actors authorized to define the immigration problematique remained thus largely unchanged. What is more, the highly intergovernmental nature of the JHA pillar allowed little room for supranational actors to influence policies. Whereas on the national level parliaments and courts have contributed to more expansive immigration policies (Freeman 1995), the marginal position of the European Parliament and the European Court of Justice in third pillar decision-making have effectively precluded them from exercising any significant influence. While the Commission has been able to wield more influence in third pillar matters, its position, too, is significantly weaker than in first pillar matters.

To begin with, the formal role of the European Parliament (EP) was limited in the sense that it could not participate in the drafting of legislation. According to the Maastricht Treaty the Council and the Commission have an obligation to 'regularly inform' and 'consult' the EP and to 'duly' take the latter's view 'into consideration'.[11] Excluded from any meaningful legislative activity, the EP has dedicated itself to the publishing of reports and opinions on its own initiative. To this end, the European Parliament set up the Committee on Civil Liberties and Internal Affairs as a new standing committee of the EP in February 1992. Although this Committee has been relatively active, the lack of any legislative powers has left the European Parliament somewhat toothless with the effect that 'parliamentary scrutiny was rather like being barked at by a puppy' (Geddes 2000: 99). The monitoring task of the European Parliament was further impeded by the fact that information on policy activities was often only forthcoming after they were decided upon (Monar 1995). In response to the semi-secret character of policy-making, the EP called for a wider interpretation of its right to being informed by the Council. To this end, the EP decided in 1993 to put forward a draft inter-institutional agreement that included the Council, Commission and the EP and which would significantly strengthen the latter's involvement in JHA policy-making (see also European Parliament 1992; European Parliament

1993a; 1993b). However, the Council had no intention (nor any legal obligation) to follow the Parliament's recommendations. In June 1994, the Council concluded that its obligation to inform the EP should be read narrowly as the obligation to forward documents on an informal basis. As a result, according to one member of Parliament, the information provided to the European Parliament did not differ fundamentally from the Council's press releases that were made available to the public (Esders 1995: 271).

The position of the European Court of Justice (ECJ) was not much different. The ECJ was not granted any jurisdiction over the policy instruments available under the provisions of Title VI on JHA. Only in the case where member states would decide to draw up conventions on matters relating to JHA, the ECJ would be allowed to interpret the provisions of the convention and to rule on its application insofar as the convention would stipulate so. However, as conventions require unanimity and, for that reason, are a little used policy instrument, the ECJ was effectively denied the influence to interpret JHA provisions.

Recalling its failure to communitarize immigration and asylum policies in the immediate period after the 1986 SEA, the Commission decided to not seek full communitarization of immigration policies in the run-up to the Maastricht Treaty. Instead, it continued its more pragmatic approach of seeking association with established intergovernmental decision-making procedures. This pragmatic style is clearly discernible in two communications, which the Commission made available to the intergovernmental negotiation process on the Maastricht Treaty (European Commission 1991a; 1991b). In these communications, the Commission pursued a double strategy. On the one hand, it underscored that the issue of immigration and asylum should be the topic of European cooperation: 'After all, in a Community where there will no longer be passport checks at the internal borders, it is essential that this new freedom is not misused to bypass the legal/administrative system established to control immigration' (European Commission 1991b: paragraph 2). On the other hand, however, the Commission is careful not to call for the communitarization of these areas. Instead, it speaks more neutrally of the need for 'joint action', 'joint measures' and 'joint responses' (European Commission 1991a: paragraph IIIA; 1991b: paragraph 12, 13).

To some degree, the Commission's strategy paid off. Article K.4 of the Maastricht Treaty stipulates that the Commission is to be fully associated with the work undertaken in the Committee of Senior Officials. Also, article K.1 specifies that cooperation on JHA is to be regarded as a 'common interest' and firmly relates cooperation on internal security to the community objective of free movement. This linkage between community objectives and immigration and asylum policies made it difficult to justify a full exclusion of the Commission. Article K.9 of the Maastricht Treaty, therefore, contained a bridge or *passerelle* from the third pillar to a communitarization of immigration policies. This article states that the Council, acting unanimously on the initiative of the Commission or a member state, could decide to apply article 100c of the Maastricht Treaty to action in the areas described in article K.1.1 to K.1.6. Theoretically, this allowed for the possibility of communitarization of immigration and asylum policies. Because of the requirement of unanimity for such a decision, the *passerelle* was however never used in practice. Yet, the very inclusion of a bridge meant that the Commission could no longer be discarded as an illegitimate intruder in the field of asylum and immigration policies. However, when asked by the Council about the possibilities of communitarizing asylum policies,[12] the Commission replied that it was too early for a communitarization. In light of the Commission's pragmatic position and considering the fact that a unanimous decision on communitarization would not be forthcoming anyway, the Commission probably opted for the best possible strategy under the circumstances. However, in doing so it also confirmed that immigration and asylum were to be considered first and foremost as the falling within the competences of internal security experts.

At the same time, the legislative position of the Commission was also significantly weakened by the fact that, in contrast to decision-making procedures in the first pillar, it had to share its right of initiative with the member states. Moreover, the rule of unanimity meant that member states always could veto any proposals made by the Commission. Adrian Fortescue, former Head of the JHA Task Force of the Commission, recalls the tenuous relationship between the Commission and the member states as follows:

> They [the member states] watch the Commission like hawks for any perceived abuse of competence or any stretching of the interpretation of the words of the Treaty ... Some of them are almost pathological to keep the Community institutions out of the process ...

> The Commission, therefore, squared the circle by setting itself the initial target of establishing its credibility, not so much through the traditional First Pillar route of tabling a number of legislative proposals but by tabling communications of a more general nature covering some of the subjects in Title VI. We saw one major advantage in such an approach as being a way of opening up the public debate on some of the subjects concerned and thus getting away from the idea that they were only discussed behind closed doors (Fortescue 1995: 21, 24–25).

Hence the Commission accepted a low-profile role in order not to be marginalized completely. By becoming a credible partner in the JHA field, the Commission hoped to lift internal security cooperation out of its previous secretive atmosphere as a means of starting a public debate about internal security cooperation. But the Commission's approach also came at a considerable cost. That is, in order to gain influence in the policy-making process it accepted the fact that immigration and asylum constituted issues of internal security. In other words, the only way for the Commission to exercise some control over JHA activities was to accept the very premise of compensatory measures as a necessary prerequisite for the internal market. Or as it states in its communication on asylum: 'The Commission considers that . . . the absence of checks at internal borders will render any control of immigration impossible. It is the Community's duty to act to prevent such perverse effects, which would hinder the achievement of objectives set out in the Single Act' (European Commission 1991a: paragraph I.12).

Thus although the Commission was not the principal driving force behind the securitization of immigration, its strategic choice to gain some influence over JHA activities nonetheless helped to enlarge the scope and reach of the European internal security field – if only by the Commission's acceptance of the compensatory measures discourse. This shift in focus was further confirmed in the institutional set-up of the Commission itself. Whereas until Maastricht the issue of immigration had been dealt with under the Commission's Social Affairs Directorate, the Commission decided to establish a five-person JHA task force within the Commission's General Secretariat. Although the task force only had limited economic and political resources (especially in comparison to Directorate Generals), it indicated the emergence of a separate 'discursive order' within the Commission. While it continued to call for more inclusive migration policies, it also began to develop a distinct 'internal security' identity with a strong focus on the control aspects of the immigration problem.

Whereas the pre-Maastricht European politics of internal security operated in a semi-secretive manner removed from public vision and public debate, the formalization and consolidation of these groups as part of the institutional structure of the EU has brought these organizations somewhat closer to public scrutiny. However, due to the intergovernmental character and the administrative culture of JHA officials, the politics of internal security is still removed from public debate, as the European Parliament, the European Court of Justice and the Commission only have had limited influence on decision-making procedures. Although the question of security has been dedramatized as a result of the inclusion of JHA, the authority to enunciate immigration is still located within the internal security professionals.

Conclusion: From Maastricht to Amsterdam

The widely shared assessment in European Studies that 'Europe since Maastricht is very much a new Europe' (Laursen 1997: 72) does not apply to the policy area of internal security in general and that of asylum and immigration in particular. Here, the Maastricht Treaty merely incorporated the already existing discourses and structures of the pre-Maastricht phase. As such, the Maastricht IGC contributed to the securitization of immigration on the European level by embedding the working structures and enunciations of informal groups such as the AHWGI, Trevi and the Coordinators' Group within the institutional structure of the EU. At the same time, these groups managed to fence off influence from supranational actors (European Commission, European Parliament) and competing functional environments (Coreper).

Yet, most member states considered the pillared structure of the EU in general and the JHA provisions more particularly as a sub-optimal compromise to accommodate the less integration inclined states (Denmark, the United Kingdom and Ireland). These political divisions were also reflected in the treaty provisions, which left many questions on the final scope of immigration and asylum policies unanswered (e.g., the *passerelle* clause). Thus while the Maastricht Treaty succeeded in providing an agreeable compromise to all member states, it was partly agreeable only because it was already laid down in the Maastricht Treaty that the institutional compromises were not written in stone. As Article N of the Maastricht Treaty states: 'A conference of the representatives of the Member States shall be convened in 1996 to examine those provisions of the Treaty for which revision is provided' (Union, European 1992). One of the areas was JHA and while Maastricht formalized the interpretation of immigration as a security issue, the policy area of JHA would undergo significant changes as a result the 1996 IGC in Amsterdam. The next chapter addresses what this has meant for the discursive struggle about the meaning of immigration.

4
Amsterdam and Beyond: Immigration and the Establishment of an AFSJ

Introduction

The Maastricht Treaty formalized internal security cooperation by bringing it within the institutional structure of the European Union. At the same time, however, the Maastricht Treaty also made clear that the JHA procedures would need to be readdressed in the 1996 IGC of Amsterdam. This chapter focuses on the Amsterdam Treaty and the JHA reforms that were introduced by that treaty and subsequent policy initiatives. Most notably, it will consider the objective to maintain and develop the EU as an AFSJ introduced by the Amsterdam Treaty and subsequently specified in the 1998 Vienna Action Plan on how best to implement the provisions relating to the AFSJ and the 1999 Tampere European Council on the AFSJ. The purpose of this chapter is to address the ways in which the Amsterdam Treaty has disrupted, transformed or reified the intersubjective structures that have informed decision-making routines on immigration since Maastricht: Which actors possess the symbolic capacity to define the 'truth' about the nature of security and immigration? Did the security professionals working under the third pillar survive the 'big bang' of the Amsterdam IGC? Or did the post-Amsterdam period actually signal the beginning of their retreat at the expense of actors less likely to view immigration in terms of security?

In answering these questions, it will be argued that Amsterdam has significantly modified decision-making routines in the area of internal security. Two developments stand out. The first is that the Amsterdam Treaty foresees in the transfer of immigration and asylum from the third pillar to the first pillar. With regard to the securitization of immigration, the move from the third to the first pillar could be expected to both strengthen and weaken the security frame. On the one hand, it could be interpreted as a strengthening of the security view, which now has travelled from the periphery (third pillar) to the core (first pillar) of the European integration project. On the other hand, it could also be interpreted as a weakening of the security frame as the first pillar has been underpinned by the liberal philosophy of free movement rather than the security philosophy of the third pillar. As the (gradual) communitarization of immigration and asylum policies changes the constellation of actors endowed with the authority to enunciate the 'truth' about immigration, it may mean that the perspective of immigration changes to one concerned more with free movement than with threat management. The second significant development is the proposal to introduce a foreign policy element into the management of immigration and asylum. Again, it could be argued that this contributes both to the securitization and desecuritization of immigration. While the introduction of foreign affairs may disentangle the question of immigration somewhat from the interpretation of internal security officials, it could also be argued that the introduction of foreign policies strengthens the security frame by giving the latter an external component.

This chapter proceeds in four sections. The next section discusses the member state negotiations and the innovations introduced by the Amsterdam Treaty in the area of JHA. It will especially focus upon the introduction of the AFSJ as a new Union objective and the ways in which this objective has impacted upon internal security cooperation in the EU. Most significantly, it will be argued that the Amsterdam IGC and the treaty objective of maintaining and developing the EU as an AFSJ has moved beyond the compensatory measures discourse by linking internal security cooperation to the feelings of insecurity of EU citizens in an attempt to bring the Union closer to its citizens. As the Amsterdam Treaty does not specify in detail how the AFSJ should be realized practically, the following section turns to a discussion of the policy-initiatives in the immediate post-Amsterdam period related to the establishment of the AFSJ (the 1998 Austrian Strategy Paper, the 1998 Vienna Action Plan and the 1999 Tampere Council Conclusions). The chapter then deals with the complementary question of how these discourses have been institutionalized in bureaucratic decision-making structures, procedures and policy budgets. Finally, the implications of the Amsterdam IGC for the (de)securitization of immigration in the EU are considered.

The AFSJ: Agenda-setting and member state negotiations

The agenda-setting phase for the Amsterdam IGC officially kicked off at the European Council in Corfu in December 1994. At this summit it was decided that the IGC would be primed by a preparatory body also known as the Reflection Group. In its capacity as the main coordinating body for the Amsterdam IGC, the group played an important role in the setting of the political agenda. Chaired by Carlos Westendorp, the group was composed of one representative from each member state, the European Commissioner Marcelino Oreja Aguirre as well as two members of the European Parliament (Elisabeth Guigou and Elmar Brok). The Corfu European Council gave the Reflection Group the rather broad mandate to express ideas relating to the provisions of the Maastricht Treaty for which a revision was foreseen (European Council 1994). As the decision-making structure of the JHA pillar was generally assumed to be part of Maastricht's 'unfinished business' (Moravcsik and Nicolaïdis 1998: 14), it was clear from the beginning that the Reflection Group would also express some ideas on reforms in the area of internal security. Hence, the 1995 European Council in Cannes asked the Reflection Group more explicitly to examine how the Union could 'provide a better response to modern demands as regards internal security, and the fields of justice and home affairs more generally' (European Council 1995a).

Internal security officials had little power to directly influence the Amsterdam IGC. Both the preparation of the IGC and the IGC negotiations were conducted by actors – the Reflection Group and the IGC representatives for the Ministers of Foreign Affairs – without a bureaucratic stake in the management of internal security threats. These actors, which were more or less composed of the same members, were encultured in the epistemic community of foreign affairs officials, either as ministers or high-ranked ambassadors.[1]

In order to facilitate the preparatory tasks of the Reflection Group, member states and community institutions were asked to submit reports on the functioning of the JHA pillar. Without exception, all of them found that cooperation on JHA was sub-optimal in terms of efficiency and accountability. Unsurprisingly, though, the member states were still divided over the question whether to communitarize parts of JHA (with immigration and asylum policies being a likely candidate) or whether to retain the *status quo* of intergovernmental decision-making.[2] The same small minority that had blocked communitarization at the Maastricht IGC – the United Kingdom, Ireland and Denmark – also resisted a transferral of decision-making competences to the Community level at the Amsterdam IGC.

Because of the differences in the positions of member states, the Council refrained from delving into the politically sensitive question of how to remedy shortcomings institutionally, although it noted that existing cooperation had worked sub-optimally (Council of the European Union 1995). By contrast, both the European Commission and the European Parliament stressed the need for more Community competences in especially the area of immigration and asylum policies, which they claimed was closely related to the Union objective of free movement (European Commission 1995; European Parliament 1995; 1996). Yet, both were also careful not to suggest a full communitarization of JHA provisions. The Commission continued to stress its role as a credible strategic partner in the area of JHA, emphasizing the all-purpose principles of transparency, accountability and efficiency without commenting too much on the question of competences: 'The Commission proposes that the shortcomings of the treaty in the fields of justice and home affairs – notably its ineffectiveness and the absence of democratic and judicial review – be remedied by setting clear objectives and providing for appropriate instruments and methods' (European Commission 1996).[3]

On the basis of all this input, the Reflection Group recommended that the IGC should focus its work on three themes: (i) to bring the Union closer to its citizens; (ii) to improve the functioning of the Union; and (iii) to enhance the Union's capacity for external action (Reflection Group 1995b). Interestingly, cooperation on JHA was included under the first category. Arguing that there was 'a clear demand on the part of the public for greater security for citizens within the Union', the Reflection Group proposed that the IGC should focus on the establishment of 'an area of freedom and security' that could reconcile the Union with its citizens:

> The Union is an area of free movement for people, goods, capital and services. Yet people's security is not sufficiently protected

> on a European scale ... Experience of the implementation of the Maastricht Treaty over the last few years shows that opportunities for effective European action are limited. Hence, the urgency for a common response at European level, following a pragmatic approach. We all agree that the Conference should strengthen the Union's capacity to protect its citizens against terrorism, drug trafficking, money laundering, exploitation of illegal immigration and other forms of internationally organized crime (Reflection Group 1995a).

The notion of a 'pragmatic approach' sidesteps the politically sensitive questions related to the communitarization of internal security issues, but the usage of the term 'urgency' stresses that immediate attention should be given to these issues. While the combination of 'pragmatism' and 'urgency' is reminiscent of the pre-Maastricht discourses on compensatory measures (see also Chapter 3), the Reflection Group nevertheless differs from the compensatory measures in one important sense. Whereas until the Amsterdam IGC the question of internal security had been discursively linked to the abolishment of internal borders, the Reflection Group articulates internal security instead as an important brick in establishing a Union close to its citizens. The referent object of European internal security has shifted from the internal market to the EU-citizens that are to move around in the AFSJ without feeling insecure.

The European Council in Madrid in December 1995 concluded that the ideas put forward by the Reflection Group constituted 'a sound basis for the work of the Conference' (European Council 1995b) and, at its 1996 meeting in Florence, asked the coming Irish Presidency to commence on 'a general outline for a Draft revision of the Treaties' to be presented at the Dublin summit in December 1996 (European Council 1996b). When the Irish Presidency started preparing a draft, roughly four options regarding reforms in JHA cooperation could be discerned.[4] The first and most radical scenario was a complete transfer of third pillar provisions to the institutional setting of the first pillar. However, with the United Kingdom, Ireland and Denmark more than reluctant to significantly change the *status quo*, this option was obviously unattainable in practice. The second alternative of a partial communitarization had the support of most member states. This option foresaw the communitarization of the areas of asylum, immigration and border controls (old articles K.1 (1–6)) and would increase the role of the supranational institutions in these areas. The third option was to introduce pragmatic improvements, while keeping the JHA pillar separated from the other pillars. The final option was simply to preserve the Maastricht *status quo*. Yet a choice for the last option seemed unlikely. After all, a majority of member states had pointed out that the Maastricht compromise was far from optimal. Even the British, the strongest defenders of the *status quo*, admitted in their Memorandum on Issues Concerning European Security that the 'IGC should examine the question of making intergovernmental cooperation under the third pillar more efficient, for example by simplifying the structure but without amending the Treaty' (see European Parliament 1997).

Building upon the Reflection Group's deliberations on the establishment of an 'area of freedom and security', the Irish Presidency eventually put forward a draft (known as 'Dublin II') in which it gave particular importance to the area of justice and home affairs (Irish Presidency 1996). Noting that there was a difference of opinion as regards the communitarization of asylum and immigration policies, the Irish cautiously argued that there was 'a measure of agreement on the use of Community methods and procedures to deal with some of the matters which until now have been dealt with by Title VI of the TEU' (cited in den Boer 2002: 519). On the basis of this 'measure of agreement' the Irish Presidency presented a draft that both foresaw the creation of an 'area of freedom, security and justice' and a new title 'free movement of persons, asylum and immigration' to be inserted in the Community section of the EU Treaty. Although not all member states supported such a move (Irish Presidency 1996: 24), the Dublin summit received the Irish draft with approval and called on the IGC to continue to 'work to reach agreement on a strengthened capacity for action in relation to visas, asylum, immigration, the crossing of external borders, the fight against drugs and international crime including terrorism, offences against children and trafficking in persons' (European Council 1996a).

As had been the case with the Maastricht Treaty, it was the responsibility of this time, the Dutch Presidency to draft the final treaty changes. With the diplomatic embarrassment of Maastricht still fresh in mind, this time the Dutch Presidency was more careful in managing the political agenda, choosing to stay close to the original Irish draft. By adopting the position that it was more crucial to begin with an identification of the objectives of JHA cooperation and the means with which to achieve them than with a discussion of where to locate competences, the Dutch Presidency successfully managed to achieve progress in the negotiating process. It followed the Irish suggestion that the supranational institutions should be given an increased role in the areas of asylum and immigration, but it also – against its own preference for the Community method – followed the Dublin suggestion that JHA provisions relating to cooperation on policing and criminal justice should remain the subject of intergovernmental decision-making in the third pillar.

On two issues, however, the Dutch Presidency moved away from the initiatives proposed by the Irish Presidency. First, where the Irish had not been very keen in propelling a discussion on flexibility in the area of JHA (probably fearing it would be left behind in the 'slower' group as a result of its association with the United Kingdom with whom it forms a Common Travel Area), the Dutch successfully reopened the discussion of a two-speed Europe to persuade states to agree with a communitarization of immigration and asylum. Eventually, a communitarization of immigration and asylum issues in a new Title IV TEC on 'free movement, asylum and immigration' was agreed upon on the basis that the United Kingdom and Ireland could 'opt out' from cooperation under this Title. The Dutch Presidency also convinced these states to agree on the incorporation of the Schengen *acquis* in the EU,[5] with the guarantee that non-Schengen members would have the right to be excluded from the Schengen *acquis*.

What, then, was the final outcome of the negotiations? First of all, the Reflection Group idea of 'an area of freedom, security and justice' obtained a central place in the new EU Treaty. In article 2 of the Treaty, the Union sets itself the objective to 'maintain and develop the Union as an area of freedom, security and justice, in which the free movement of persons is assured in conjunction with appropriate measures with respect to external border controls, asylum, immigration and the prevention and combating of crime' (European Union 2002). Although the objective is clear, the practical provisions towards the achievement of this objective were located in different parts of the Amsterdam Treaty. The provisions on police and judicial cooperation remained the subject of intergovernmental decision-making under new Title VI TEU (articles 29–45), while the issues of immigration, asylum and border control moved to the new first pillar Title IV on 'Visas, Asylum, Immigration and other Policies related to Free Movement of Persons'. The newly established first pillar title is aimed 'at ensuring the free movement of persons ... in conjunction with directly related flanking measures with respect to external border controls, asylum and immigration' (European Union 2002: article 61(a)). It was decided however that the provisions falling under this title would be communitarized only gradually. In the first 5 years after ratification of the Amsterdam Treaty (from 1 May 1999 to 30 April 2004) the Commission would still have to share the right of initiative with the member states. After 5 years, the Commission gained the capacity to propose directives and binding measures to the Council, which decides on their acceptability by unanimous vote, unless the Council votes unanimously to shift to qualified majority voting. As regards the incorporation of Schengen, the part of the Schengen *acquis* referring to immigration, border control and asylum has been integrated under Title IV TEC, whereas the other provisions were incorporated as part of third pillar cooperation.

In short, communitarization could only be achieved at the price of differentiated integration in the area of internal security. But although the result is a fragmented Treaty 'baroquely decorated with facultative arrangements, time-clauses and protocols' (den Boer and Corrado 2000: 398), the objective of the maintenance and development of the EU as an AFSJ gave an enormous impetus to internal security. The purpose of creating such an area was to provide EU citizens with a high level of safety, which in turn was regarded as an indispensable step towards bringing the Union closer to its citizens. However, the Amsterdam Treaty does not specify in detail how the AFSJ should be defined practically. Therefore, the Cardiff European Council in June 1998, almost a year before the official ratification of the Amsterdam Treaty, called on the Council and the Commission to draw up an action plan 'on how best to implement the provisions of the Treaty of Amsterdam on an area of freedom, security and justice' (European Council 1998b). An important element in the immediate post-Amsterdam period, therefore, has been to specify the meaning of the AFSJ and the actors responsible for its maintenance and development.

Beyond Amsterdam: Establishing the AFSJ

The linkage of internal security to the every-day life of individual citizens has become inscribed as a core objective to be achieved by the European Union. The Vienna Action Plan on how best to implement the provisions of the Amsterdam Treaty establishing an area of freedom, security and justice (adopted by the European Council on 7 December 1998) builds upon this linkage in its attempt to turn the AFSJ into a concrete programme. In a sense, the Action Plan follows the legal distinction of the Amsterdam Treaty, where immigration and asylum are located in Title IV TEC on free movement of persons, while internal security questions are dealt with under Title VI TEU. In a similar fashion, the 1998 Vienna Action Plan considers the questions of asylum and immigration under the heading of 'An Area of Freedom' (paragraphs 6–8), while questions such as organized crime, drugs and policing are dealt with under the separate heading of 'An Area of Security' (paragraphs 9–14). However, the separation between the two loses its meaning when one considers in more detail the ways in which the Action Plan has given a practical meaning to the concepts of security and freedom. Having established that one of its aims is to reflect on the 'general approach and philosophy inherent in the concept of an area of freedom, security and justice', the Action Plan goes on to outline the link between freedom, security and justice as follows:

> Freedom loses much of its meaning if it cannot be enjoyed in a secure environment and with the full backing of a system of justice in which all Union citizens and residents can have confidence. These three inseparable concepts have one common denominator – people – and one cannot be achieved in full without the other two (European Council 1998a: paragraph 5).

Here, the Action Plan thus closely follows the Reflection Group in elevating the citizen into the central referent object of security. Prior to the Amsterdam IGC the internal market had been the main referent object for security, the post-Amsterdam stress on public feelings of anxiety stresses instead an individual's right to live a life free from threats. Thus, the Action Plan defines the meaning of freedom as entailing more than just the right to free movement:

> Freedom in the sense of free movement of people within the European Union remains a fundamental objective of the Treaty, and one to which the flanking measures associated with the concepts of security and justice must make their essential contribution. The Schengen achievement has shown the way and provides the foundation on which to build. However, the Treaty of Amsterdam

> also opens the way to giving 'freedom' a meaning beyond free movement of people across internal borders. It is also freedom to live in a law-abiding environment in the knowledge that public authorities are using everything in their individual and collective power ... to combat and contain those who seek to deny or abuse that freedom (European Council 1998a: paragraph 6).

To realize the objective of freedom practically, the EU has adopted facilitating measures such as the creation of the internal market, the introduction of a European citizenship and ostensibly more mundane regulations such as the introduction of a European health card. All these measures have enabled individuals to be recognized as legal subjects and to enact their individual freedom across borders (Barry 1993; 1994). By removing barriers and limitations to movement, the EU has thus created conditions in which individuals have obtained a 'freedom to'. With the Action Plan the *freedom to* live in a law-abiding environment is in turn operationalized as the *freedom from* those who are identified as abusers of that freedom. As all but the most radical liberals would insist that the exercise of freedom should be unlimited, the choice between freedom and security is always a delicate trade-off. On the one hand, freedom has to be fostered. On the other hand, absolute freedom of movement has to be tempered in order to make sure that the free movement of some does not encroach upon the free movement of others. Internal security measures and risk management are invoked as defensive mechanisms to protect individuals from encroachment by others. The optimal exercise of freedom within the EU does not only depend upon facilitating measures that seek to establish the optimal conditions under which individuals can conduct their own freedom, but also on security measures that restrict and control improper forms of the conduct of freedom. Or as António Vitorino, the first European Commissioner for Justice and Home Affairs put it: 'Security ... is a means of achieving freedom. Security and freedom go hand in hand.'[6] His view that security is an important element in crafting freedom is also expressed in the Vienna Action Plan, which states explicitly that '[t]he full benefits of any area of freedom will never be enjoyed unless they are exercised in an area where people can feel safe and secure' (European Council 1998a: paragraph 9).

To increase the capacity to control those that 'deny' or 'abuse' freedom, the Vienna Action Plan also refers to external relations as a possible component in the management of migration flows (European Council 1998a: paragraph 22). The objective is to manage the conduct of freedom between itself and the external environment through the deployment of instruments normally associated with the domain of foreign affairs (e.g., trade relations, economic development, human rights). The linkage between, on the one hand, the control of immigration and, on the other, foreign policy objectives has raised the important question of what would be the exact balance between the two. Would immigration and asylum policies become part of foreign policies or would justice and home affairs be geared with an external dimension? Would (parts of) immigration and asylum be moved to a new institutional and policy framework? Or would it entail an upgrade and expansion of the already existing policies and institutions within the JHA context?

In the direct aftermath of the Amsterdam IGC, the 1998 Austrian Presidency took a first step towards the formulation of immigration policy as a 'transformed foreign approach' (van Selm 2002).[7] In its capacity as Council Presidency, Austria put forward a Strategy Paper on immigration and asylum in which it seeks to expand internal security objective to the external domain: 'The reduction of migratory pressure calls for a coordinated policy which extends far beyond the narrow field of policy on aliens, asylum, immigration and border controls, and also covers international relations and development aid' (Austrian Presidency 1998: paragraph 51, see also paragraph 40). Drawn up within the bureaucratic context of the Austrian Ministry of Justice, the Austrian Strategy Paper was clear about the internal security-foreign policy nexus: External action was to be seen first and foremost as an element in the management of the abusive conduct of freedom.

Following the view that the Union should strengthen the external dimension of its immigration and asylum policies, the Dutch Foreign Ministry proposed to create a body responsible for the foreign policy aspects of immigration policies in 1998. On the domestic level, the Dutch already had a few years experience in coordinating policies on foreign affairs, refugees and immigration (Boswell 2003b: 629). Drawing upon its domestic experiences, the Dutch delegation to the Council put forward a proposal to create a horizontal task force on asylum and migration in order to establish a common, integrated, cross-pillar approach to immigration (Dutch Delegation to the Council 1998). The proposal was accepted and a cross-pillar task force with the name

High-Level Working Group on Asylum and Migration (HLWG) was established. In accordance with the tasks proposed in the note by the Dutch delegation, the HLWG was given the mandate to draw up a list of the most important countries of origin and transit for which cross-pillar actions plans should be drafted. The following countries and regions were selected: Afghanistan/Pakistan; Albania and its neighbouring region; Morocco; Somalia; and Sri Lanka. In addition, the HLWG would also take up and assess the already existing action plan on the influx of migrants from Iraq. According to the terms of reference that were endorsed by the General Affairs Council of 25 January 1999, the HLWG would, among others, analyze the causes of influx, put forward suggestions aimed at strengthening the common strategy for development with the country concerned, identify humanitarian needs and investigate proposals for the intensification of political and diplomatic dialogue with selected countries (Coreper 1999).

In comparison to the Austrian Strategy Paper – which was drawn up by internal security bureaucrats and which regarded foreign affairs first and foremost as a brick in the wall of internal security – the HLWG pursued a more genuine foreign affairs objective, although it was also concerned with security-related issues such as border control and readmission agreements. The 1999 Tampere European Council on the creation of an AFSJ built upon the HLWG and reflected a similar balance between JHA objectives and foreign policy objectives. Thus the Tampere Conclusions call for a 'comprehensive approach' to immigration and asylum:

> The European Union needs a comprehensive approach to migration addressing political, human rights and development issues in countries and regions of origin and transit. This requires combating poverty, improving living conditions and job opportunities, preventing conflicts and consolidating democratic states and ensuring respect for human rights, in particular rights of minorities, women and children. To that end, the Union as well as Member States are invited to contribute, within their respective competences under the Treaties, to a greater coherence of internal and external policies of the Union. Partnership with third countries concerned will also be a key element for the success of such a policy, with a view to promoting co-development (European Council 1999: paragraph 11).

However, in a later passage the Tampere Conclusions seem to move away from the foreign affairs view towards a more security-oriented view:

> The European Union underlines that all competences and instruments at the disposal of the Union, and in particular, in external relations must be used in an integrated and consistent way to build the area of freedom, security and justice. Justice and Home Affairs concerns must be integrated in the definition and implementation of other Union policies and activities' (European Council 1999: paragraph 59).

In short, then, EU policy-initiatives, documents and discourses have oscillated uncomfortably between foreign policy objectives on the one hand and those of justice and home affairs on the other. The question of the balance between the two is a crucial one for the struggle about the meaning of immigration, as a transferral of the competences to deal with immigration from internal security experts to foreign affairs officials can make a difference to the way in which immigration is interpreted. As the involvement of foreign affairs officials entails the mobilization of different institutions (e.g., development workers, diplomats, external security professionals), this means that other forms of knowledge are involved in the social construction of immigration. For instance, foreign affairs officials are generally predisposed to focus on the social, political and economic situation in a country and the implications thereof for international stability. For them, therefore, immigration flows are not the central concern of policy-making. The latter only enters the equation as one of the indicators – together with, for example, terrorist activity, economic underdevelopment, authoritarian government, human rights violations and regional conflicts – for 'state failure', that is, the inability or unwillingness of states to provide and develop a stable domestic economic and political system.[8] As such, they seek not so much to govern immigrants *per se* but rather what are perceived to be the root causes of immigration (see Niessen 1999). Actually, foreign policy objectives can sometimes even conflict with those of justice and home affairs officials. Promoting economic development is, at least in the short or medium term, likely to increase rather than decrease migration. Industrialization uproots existing economic and social structures with the result that some individuals who can no longer uphold their traditional livelihood may have to consider migration as an alternative life strategy. At the same time, economic aid may empower people to migrate, as previously these individuals were without the financial means to do so (European Commission 2002). Economic development may also create new economic and political fault lines that can propel or reinforce social conflicts (ethnic, religious, political) and, consequently, produce a higher percentage of refugees trying to escape these conflicts (see Zolberg, Suhrke et al. 1989; Chimni 1998).

The question to which degree Amsterdam has transformed, reified or perhaps even strengthened the security frame that has informed decision-making routines on immigration since Maastricht, therefore, requires an additional discussion of the post-Amsterdam working structures and the turf battles that take place on that level. While political discourses and political imaginations of the area of freedom, security and justice are relevant, it is also necessary to examine the degree to which the different political discourses are grounded and reflected in bureaucratic decision-making structures and procedures.

Post-Amsterdam bureaucratic working structures

As was shown in the previous chapter, the Maastricht Treaty left the pre-Maastricht decision-making structures relatively intact. Rather than creating new working structures, it integrated the informal working groups on security within the bureaucratic landscape of the Union. Yet, as all member states agreed that the third pillar decision-making procedures were inefficient and unaccountable, it was clear from the outset that these would have to be reconsidered at Amsterdam. The provisions relating to the establishment of the EU as an AFSJ and the transfer of security provisions gave further rise to speculation about the status of internal security professionals and the allocation of symbolic authority to speak immigration. Since traditionally the first pillar has been underpinned by the liberal philosophy of free movement rather than the security philosophy of the third pillar, the institutional inscription of immigration in the former could also be believed to disrupt the problematization of immigration in terms of security.

Similarly, the creation of the HLWG and the involvement of foreign affairs officials may have well disrupted the problematization of immigration in terms of security in favour of a problematization of immigrants as the victim of social, political and economic mismanagement in countries of destination. The question, then, is whether or not the security professionals working under the third pillar also survived the 'big bang' of the Amsterdam IGC! Did the post-Amsterdam period actually signal the beginning of their retreat at the expense of actors less likely to view immigration in terms of security?

The European Commission

The transfer of immigration and asylum policies to Title IV TEC was followed by significant reforms in the Commission working structure. To a large degree, these reforms reflect the above described tensions and dynamics between, on the one hand, security and freedom and, on the other, internal security and foreign policy objectives. As regards the freedom–security nexus, the JHA task force established within the context of the Secretariat-General of the Council was understaffed in relation to the Commission's larger and better equipped Directorate Generals for policy-making in other areas related to free movement. Whereas the Task Force on JHA employed on average 46.5 full-time employees in 1998, Directorate-General V on employment and Directorate-General XV on the internal market employed 467.25 and 275.15 employees respectively (European Commission 1999: 115, 119, 122). Hence, in the period immediately following the signing of the Amsterdam Treaty, the political priority of establishing an AFSJ was not mirrored by a relocation of more Commission resources to JHA. What is more, there were no definite plans on how to adapt the Commission's working structure to the new objective of the establishment and development of the EU as an AFSJ. As a consequence, the Commission's resources did not match the political priorities of the Amsterdam Treaty. During the Amsterdam IGC and the immediate period afterwards, JHA cooperation did not even constitute an autonomous area within the Commission but fell under the responsibility of the Swedish Commissioner Anita Gradin, who was also responsible for financial control. In addition, Anita Gradin was generally not regarded as being an active initiator of policies relating to the area of justice and home affairs (Esders 1995). As a new Commission was not envisaged to commence until 2000, the lack of human resources in JHA seemed to imply that the question of immigration and asylum would have to be integrated in the less security-oriented Directorate Generals relating to the question of free movement.

However, when the entire Commission resigned in 1999 as a result of a financial mismanagement case, the Commission obtained an unexpected opportunity to strengthen its bureaucratic profile in the area of JHA. Indeed, arguing that its structures no longer corresponded to the Treaty priorities, the Commission maintained in July 1999 that the 'Task Force for Justice and Home Affairs in the Secretariat-General is insufficient to meet the requirements of the Treaty (it requires a certain autonomy to give it a higher profile and, in addition, some of its new responsibilities are currently dealt with by other DGs/departments)' (European Commission 1999: 28). Concomitantly, one of the first decisions taken by the new Prodi Commission was to appoint, for the first time in the history of the Union, a Commissioner responsible solely for the area of JHA. This post was given to the Portuguese Commissioner António Vitorino who, contrary to Anita Gradin, had significant experience in the field of JHA as a result of his former function as chairman for the European Parliament's Civil Liberties and Internal Affairs Committee. His ability to actively pursue policies in the area of JHA was further strengthened by the creation of a new Directorate General for Justice and Home Affairs (DG-JHA), which replaced the much smaller Task Force on JHA in September 1999 (see Figure 4.1). The creation of a DG-JHA carried important symbolic importance in the sense that it signalled that from now on the AFSJ would be an autonomous policy area within the Commission. The creation of a new DG-JHA also proved significant in the concrete terms of human resources. The workers employed in the area of JHA multiplied by three within the first year, which meant that the new Directorate-General could start to take over some of the issues pertaining to cross-border movement that before had been dealt with by other Directorate-Generals. Although the new DG-JHA continued along the lines of the Task Force – with Adrian Fortescue, *Conseiller hors classe* of the old Task Force, becoming the new head of the DG-JHA – the new DG-JHA also incorporated senior officials from other directorates on cross-border movement. This contributed to resolving the question of functional competition with other DGs on the question of free movement (Uçarer 2001: 12).

The role of the Commission in establishing an area of freedom, security and justice was further strengthened by the 1999 Tampere

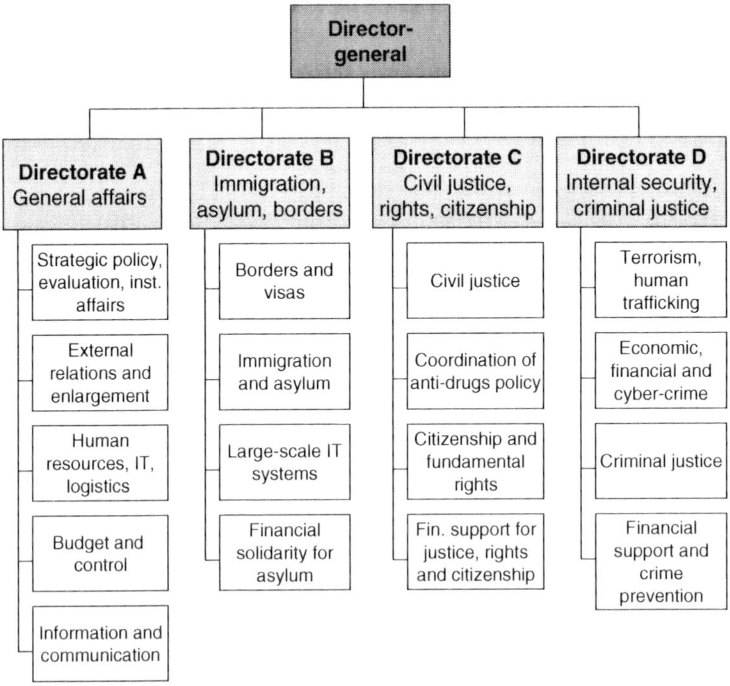

Figure 4.1 The Directorate General Justice and Home Affairs (DG-JHA)*
Note: * The DG-JHA has since beeen renamed DG Freedom, Security and Justice

Council, where the European leaders called on the Commission to monitor a timetable of progress with regard to each goal outlined in the Tampere Conclusions. With the aim of sustaining the momentum of post-Tampere cooperation, the JHA Commissioner developed a so-called 'scoreboard' of measures to be taken in the field of JHA. In managing the scoreboard and, hence, in evaluating progress the Commission has thus been given a significant leverage over the agenda-setting process in the area of justice and home affairs. Even though Commissioner Vitorino was quick to argue that the scoreboard should not be seen as a set of legislative proposals (something which would no doubt have upset some of the member states), bringing together the various goals and deadlines of internal security cooperation nevertheless functioned 'to exert pressure on areas where progress is lagging behind, in order to repeat the successful experience made with the White Paper for the Internal Market' (JHA Council 1999).

In terms of balancing the objectives of freedom and security, however, the strengthened position of the Commission has not led to a less security-dominated view of immigrants. To the contrary, the area of JHA has been given a more prominent place in the Commission working structure which has occurred at the detriment of other Directorate-Generals, who saw their policy-making competences (and in some cases also staff members) in the area of cross-border movement transferred to the new Directorate-General for Justice and Home Affairs.

With respect to the trade-off between foreign affairs and internal security concerns, the Vienna Action Plan and especially the Tampere Conclusions clearly instructed the Commission to contribute recommendations on how best to develop the external dimension. However, with significant disagreement between the different Directorate-Generals within the Commission, this was easier said than done. Obviously, the newly created DG-JHA argued for a wide-ranging reorientation of external relations. However, Commission officials working in the Directorate-Generals for development and external relations were less willing to make external relations subordinate to the management of immigration flows. They feared that such a reorientation would disturb the objectives of foreign and development policy. For instance, making development aid conditionally dependent upon immigration flows might result in more aid being given to countries with less economic need, but with a higher percentage of emigrants. Targeting those who were most willing to move, therefore, was feared to be to the detriment of those who were most vulnerable in social and economic terms. Such a distortion was also likely to occur within a country; emigrants are often young and male, whereas the Union's external goals are to empower marginalized groups, especially women and children. As a result, the DGs for development and external policy resisted a wholesale reorientation of development policies and objectives. Protecting their turf, they argued instead for a narrower external dimension that was more in line with JHA objectives. The result, as Boswell concludes, is paradoxical insofar as the attempts by external and development policy officials 'to avoid migration prevention goals into development and external relations, the DGs for development and external relations were effectively aligning themselves with the externalization of [the] control agenda favoured by the JHA Council' (Boswell 2003b: 633).

As a consequence, the Commission failed to make any concrete proposals along the lines suggested by the Tampere Conclusions. At the European Council of Laeken in December 2001, when the Commission evaluated progress on the Tampere scoreboard, it showed that the Commission had focused predominantly on restrictive measures in the external dimension, moving away from its earlier efforts to develop a 'root causes' approach to immigration. Instead, the Commission satisfied itself by pointing out that this area was already covered by the HLWG. In 2002, however, the Commission resumed its activities to integrate foreign policies and justice and home affairs. Undoubtedly, an important reason for returning to this question was that the issue continued to be on the political agenda. For instance, the Laeken Presidency Conclusions reiterated that a 'true common asylum and immigration policy implies the ... integration of the policy on migratory flows into the European Union's foreign policy' (European Council 2001: 11). The Seville European Council of 21–22 June 2002 stated that 'in accordance with the Tampere European Council conclusions, an integrated, comprehensive and balanced approach to tackling the root causes of illegal immigration must remain in the European Union's constant long-term objective. With this in mind, the European Council points out that closer economic cooperation, trade expansion, development assistance and conflict prevention are all means of promoting economic prosperity in the countries concerned and thereby reducing the underlying causes of migration flows' (European Council 2002: 10). According to Boswell (2003b: 634), this persuaded the Directorate-General on external relations and development to reconsider its negative position if they did not want to lose initiative to justice and home affairs officials.

The renewed efforts led to the production of a Commission communication on 'Integrating migration issues in the European Union's relations with third countries' (European Commission 2002). In this communication, the Commission returns to the issue of a root cause approach to immigration as a means of dealing with 'the concerns connected with the consequences of the migratory phenomenon, such as they are expressed within the European Union in recent years' (European Commission 2002: 7). Although the foreign affairs agenda is driven by worries about the adverse effects of immigration on the EU and its member states, the communication represents a careful compromise between justice and home affairs officials on the one hand and external and development policy officials on the other. The Commission communication is careful to stress that the including migration policy in third country relations should not upset original development objectives:

> The overall framework of the development policy is by now well established and should not be overturned by new priority areas ... To ensure coherence between the Community development and migration policy it is necessary to assess systematically the relationship between migration issues and the priority sectors and cross-cutting concerns of EU development policy, and to identify actions were appropriate (European Commission 2002: 21).

But while the communication to a considerable extent meets the concerns of external and development policy officials – for instance, by stressing that attempts to manage migration flows should be financed with new funds rather than already existing development funds – Boswell's conclusion that '[c]ooperation on migration management, including readmission agreements, border control and combating illegal migration, is treated as largely subordinate to the central strategy of reducing migratory pressures through development aid' (Boswell 2003b: 636) seems incorrect.

First of all, if one looks at the financial resources available at the Community level, it is obvious that most of these resources are directed not towards the objective of fighting the root causes of migration but, rather, focus on migration management. Although the budget available for policies on asylum, immigration and management of external frontiers was budgeted to rise from €29,559,894 in 1998 to €59,600,000 in 2003, no money is reserved for addressing root causes. Instead, almost half the money was allocated to a European Refugee Fund to share the burden of asylum-seekers and to promote voluntarily repatriation, while the rest of the money is reserved for the funding of Eurodac, the establishment of a European Migration Monitoring Centre, integration of third country nationals and the training of officials in the area of justice and home affairs (European Commission 2002: Annex 1). With respect to the financial resources for external aid linked to the migration issue, only 13.01% out of a total sum of €934,468,288 is reserved for development, while 47.34% is allocated to the management of migration flows (e.g., management of borders, combating illegal immigration). General JHA programmes (training, cooperation programmes, etc.) absorb 10.33% of the budget with the remaining 20.72% going to humanitarian relief and crisis help (European Commission 1999: Annex 2). In addition, in 2001 a new budget line (B7-667) of €10 million was created to support cooperation with third countries in the area of migration (European Commission 2001). This budget line reflects the priority given to issues of control and repression of immigration flows, as it focuses on migration management, the fight against illegal immigration, and voluntary return and efficient execution of readmission obligations. The budget, although still relatively small, has been doubled to approximately €20 million in 2003.

Second, there is some tension between the European Council and the Commission as to what should take precedence. Whereas the Commission's 1999 communication, reflecting its internal bureaucratic struggles, does call for a somewhat more balanced approach, the 2001 Laeken and 2002 Seville European Councils have rather stressed the control aspects of immigration. For example, whereas the Commission communication calls for genuine partnership with the EU and appreciates the problems third countries may meet in managing migration flows, the Seville European Council considers instead that it is:

> necessary to carry out a systematic assessment of relations with third countries which do not cooperate in combating illegal immigration. That assessment will be taken into account in relations between the European Union and its Member States and the countries concerned, in all relevant areas. Insufficient cooperation by a country could hamper the establishment of closer relations between that country and the Union (European Council 2002: 11).

Also here, the allocation of budgets point to a favouring of internal security measures. To this end, in March 2004 a multi-annual financial framework was put into operation for the years 2004–2008 which aimed to provide financial and technical aid to third countries in the area of migration and asylum. A total amount of €250 million is made available 'to provide a specific additional response to the needs of third countries in their efforts to manage more effectively all aspects of migratory flows, and in particular to stimulate third countries' readiness to conclude readmission agreements, and to assist them in coping with the consequences of such agreements' (Council of the European Union 2004). The amount will be spent on internal security related measures such as information campaigns, development of legislation, exchange of information and know-how, staff training, capacity-building in the areas of border controls and security of travel documents and visas, technical and operational assistance, purchase of equipment and supplies, reintegration of returnees and resettlement programs, and assistance in the negotiation by the third countries concerned of their own readmission agreements with relevant countries.

The Council structure: SCIFA, Schengen and the HLWG

The communitarization of asylum and immigration policies seemed to imply that the Council procedures would become more like the three-tiered structure (Council, Coreper, and working groups) for other policy areas falling under the Community method. Much, at least, had already pointed in that direction during the agenda-setting process of the Amsterdam IGC, where member states expressed their dissatisfaction with post-Maastricht JHA decision-making structures (see Reflection Group 1995b). Revisions to ensure a more effective, efficient and accountable decision-making process were therefore likely to take place. For example, Austria proposed to do away with at least one level of decision-making (European Parliament 1997) and in the early months of the IGC negotiations it was even discussed to abolish the K.4 Committee as the main coordinating body for internal security questions. While it was eventually decided that the K.4 Committee would remain in place (Monar 1997: 336), the three Steering Groups operating directly under the K.4 Committee were abandoned already during the IGC process, when these groups were *de facto* sidelined by the decision of the Luxembourg Presidency to no longer draw upon their expertise (de Lobkowicz 2002: 58). Since the Amsterdam Treaty did not specify any legal obligation to establish a coordinating body of senior officials for policies relating to the free movement of persons, it seemed to further contribute to the decoupling of internal security experts from the issues of immigration and asylum.

It was decided, for instance, that the K.4 Committee would no longer be the coordinating body for policies that were transferred from the third pillar to Title IV TEC (immigration, asylum and border control). Instead, the role of the K.4 Committee (renamed the 'Article 36 Committee') was limited to coordinating policies falling under the third pillar (see Figure 4.2).

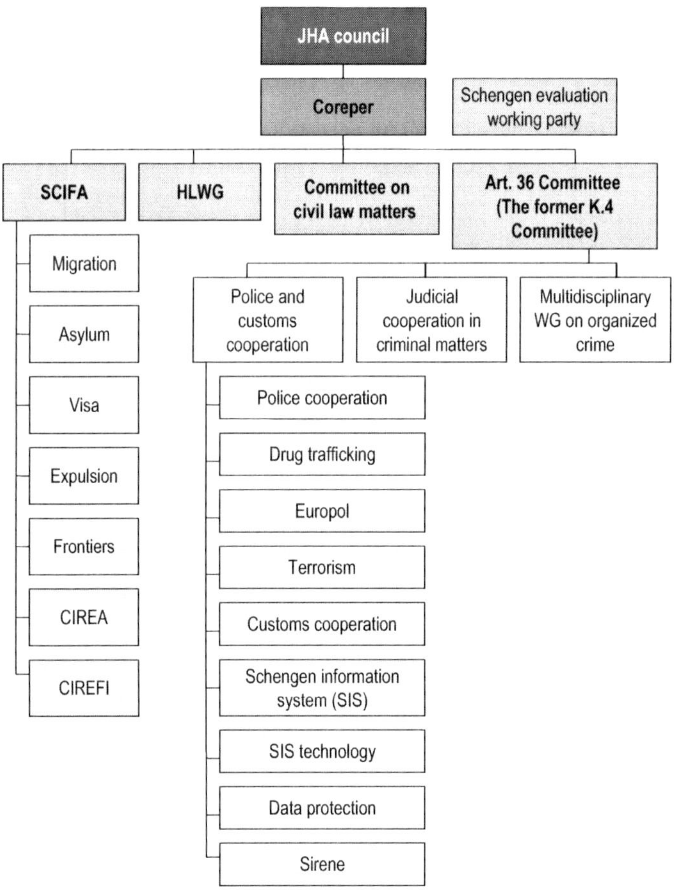

Figure 4.2 Post-Amsterdam Council working structures on asylum and immigration
Source: Adapted from Monar (2000, 2002)

To some extent, the reduction of security professionals in the Council structure could be expected to break their hegemony. However, when the working structures of the Council were discussed in more detail by member states during April and May 1999, it became apparent that several member states were reluctant to give up their discretion in the area of immigration and asylum (de Lobkowicz 2002). As a result, the member states decided to set up the Strategic Committee for Immigration, Frontiers and Asylum (SCIFA) in-between the level of Coreper and the individual working groups. Since the members represented in SCIFA were senior officials from justice and home affairs departments, the result was a four-level structure where internal security experts remained the key actors. Moreover, the working groups working directly under SCIFA were similar to the working groups that had operated under the auspices of the K.4 Committee in the post-Maastricht framework. Although the SCIFA – as the K.4 Committee before it – has no direct access to the JHA Council, the creation of SCIFA in 1999 was a strong sign of continuing justice and home affairs influence. In addition, the Amsterdam Treaty foresaw in the incorporation of the Schengen working groups, which meant that new security professionals were attached to the Council working groups. The incorporation of Schengen within the Council working structure meant that justice and home affairs gained significantly in terms of operational quality (the Schengen Information System and several working procedures and arrangements such as the stationing of liaison officers and police cooperation).

Although legally the incorporation of Schengen led to complex arrangements, institutionally there were fewer problems. The Central Group, which performed the central coordinating role in the Schengen structure, was removed. But, since the members of the Central Group were often the same as those represented in the K.4 Committee, they would continue to play a role in the Article 36 Committee under the third pillar. Representatives of individual working groups of Schengen were incorporated in similar, already existing working groups either under SCIFA or under the new Article 36 Committee. Initially, there were some problems as to where the working groups relating to the Schengen Information System should be located. Some member states argued that the SIS was mainly an instrument for police cooperation and therefore should be placed within the institutional context of the third pillar; other member states argued that the SIS played an important role in the management of (illegal) migration flows through the storage of important data on false and stolen documents as well as on illegal immigrants (Ministerie van Buitenlandse Zaken 1999). While it was decided to give the SIS a legal basis under Title VI on police cooperation, the discussion about where to incorporate the SIS nevertheless illustrates that the legal separation between first and third pillar issues is not necessarily mirrored on the institutional level.

The communitarization of immigration and asylum policies did not entail the expected shift towards a more central role for Coreper as the main policy coordinator in the area of immigration and asylum. However, Coreper's position has been somewhat strengthened as a result of the creation of the inter-pillar HLWG which reports directly to Coreper (and not to SCIFA). More specifically, as the HLWG was established when the EU was still operating under the Maastricht structures, the Council asked Coreper and not the K.4 Committee to set out the terms of references for the HLWG. Although de Lobkowicz notes that the creation of the high-level group SCIFA is a peculiar step considering the establishment of the HLWG only a couple of month earlier (de Lobkowicz 2002), the establishment of SCIFA can thus also be seen as an attempt to secure a dominant position for internal security professionals, which were confronted with an increasing activity of Coreper and the HLWG in 'their' policy area.[9] Moreover, if one looks at the composition of the HLWG in more detail, it appears less inter-pillar as could be expected from its mandate. The HLWG is compromised mainly of civil servants from the national ministries responsible for justice and home affairs, which are represented in all member state delegations to HLWG meetings in Brussels. Only the Netherlands and Sweden send delegations headed by foreign affairs representatives, while foreign affairs officials are also included in the delegations from Spain and the United Kingdom. The remaining 11 states send justice and home affairs officials only (see van Selm 2002).

Nevertheless, the creation of SCIFA entailed that two coordinating bodies on immigration existed: One inter-pillar body (which turned out not be so inter-pillar after all) with the objective to implement a comprehensive approach to immigration and a body that solely projected the view of internal security experts. Unlike SCIFA, however, the HLWG could not draw upon the expertise of working groups under the working structures put up under the JHA Council. Instead, the HLWG depended on the external relations community to implement development policies and foreign policies to address the root causes of migration. However, Commission officials dealing with the external relations were unwilling to participate in the action plans of the HLWG, complaining that they had been largely excluded from drafting these plans (Boswell 2003b: 631). As the HLWG operated under the auspices of the JHA Council and because it consisted almost exclusively of JHA officials, the external policy community feared a distortion of development policies. Although the action plans were intended to establish a cross-pillar approach with respect to the situation in a number of important countries of origin or transit, they were criticized by non-governmental organizations, the European Parliament and Morocco (which was one of the partner countries) for a lack of dialogue and partnership (Amnesty International 1999; European Parliament 2000a; 2000b).

The foreign policy element was further undermined due to the manifest emphasis of the on security-related measures in the HLWG, which clearly reflect the JHA view on immigration. The plans' main focus was on the conclusion and implementation of readmission agreements, but it also included proposals with regard to sending liaison officers to airports in order to improve gate checks, support for the adoption of visa requirements by the target countries for third country nationals, technical and financial support to the target countries for the identification and detection of criminal trafficking networks, strategies for early detection of false documents, the organization of information campaigns in the target countries to advise on migration options and to warn against the consequences of illegally entering EU member states, assistance and training of asylum and migration officials and border authorities, and increasing reception and protection capacities in the region of origin. As such, the action plans made clear that the security of the EU member states and not the economic, political and social development of target countries would be the major concern of the HLWG.

To sum up, both the working structure of the Commission as well as that of the Council reflect to a considerable degree the world view of internal security professionals. The possibility for desecuritization – created by the call for a comprehensive approach and the transferral of immigration and asylum issues to the first pillar – has been effectively counterbalanced by justice and home affairs officials. The erection of a DG-JHA within the Commission has significantly strengthened the security frame within the Commission at the expense of other DGs dealing either with issues related to free movement or with foreign and development policy. Within the Council structure, internal security professionals have managed to retain their central place due to the creation of SCIFA on the one hand and the 'colonization' of the HLWG on the other. The incorporation of the Schengen working groups has further added to the dominant security frame. Whereas the Maastricht Treaty formalized and institutionalized the security enunciations of internal security professionals, the Amsterdam Treaty has gone further. It has expanded the scope of the internal security field through the political creation of an AFSJ, which is to be maintained through the deployment of security measures in, among others, the area of immigration and asylum. Thus while the 'big bang' of the Amsterdam IGC did provide some opportunities for dislocating the security frame, internal security officials have nonetheless been effective in shaping the 'problem' of immigration.

The normalization of security: Implications for immigration

The link between threat management and public opinion has given the impression of a more democratic form of security politics where the supply of threat management is made dependent upon public concerns rather than upon expert judgements. Security is formulated not so much in terms of urgency and priority but as the product of popular will (as, for instance, expressed through *Eurobarometer* opinion polls about the fears and anxieties of EU-citizens). Indeed, already during the agenda-setting phase of the Amsterdam IGC, the Reflection Group had identified that the Union should 'give priority to the "real" problems, i.e. those which preoccupy Europeans the most', while claiming that '[t]here is a clear demand on the part of the public for greater security within the Union' (Reflection Group 1995b). This was confirmed by the Amsterdam Treaty and the Vienna Action Plan. Also the subsequent transferral of immigration and asylum to the first pillar has contributed to the normalization of EU immigration policies. It entailed that immigration and asylum politics would become more susceptible to public scrutiny and the involvement of non-security actors such as the European Commission and the European Parliament.

However, the fact that security politics has become more transparent does not automatically mean that it is also more democratic. For instance, the inclusion of the legally binding texts of Schengen in the EU *acquis* without formal consultation with the European Parliament or national parliaments raises deep concerns about the democratic legitimacy of threat management. The same can be said for the fact that the security professionals who played a dominant role in the third pillar have managed to hold on to central positions in the Union's post-Amsterdam working structure (e.g., SCIFA, HLWG and the Schengen working groups). Indeed, one cannot but notice the slightly ironic fact that what started out as informal cooperation between security experts in semi-secretive platforms as Trevi, Schengen and the AHWGI outside the sphere of democratic decision-making is now viewed as a key ingredient for improving the legitimacy of the EU!

On balance, though, the Amsterdam Treaty has inscribed the management of immigration more firmly within a framework of communicative action and public legitimation. If internal security cooperation had been operating in the margins of the integration project (the third pillar of the Maastricht Treaty) or even outside the official integration project (the pre-Maastricht platforms of Schengen, Trevi and the AHWGI), the objective of the development and maintenance of the EU as an AFSJ has given internal security cooperation a visible place in the European integration process.

How, then, do these developments fit with the Copenhagen School's notion of securitization as an exceptional discourse that bypasses the normal rules of democracy? According to the Copenhagen School, the normalization of security policies also entails a desecuritization of immigration by bringing the latter out of the sphere of extraordinary measures and into the sphere of democratic decision-making. The normalization of immigration policies, the argument goes, means that the security discourse will be rendered more susceptible to claims put forward in counter discourses. The move from security to politics means that alternative framings of immigration are no longer silenced and marginalized by appeals to 'survival' and 'existential threats' that override all other arguments. Contra the Copenhagen School, however, our discussion shows that the normalization of immigration policies has not been followed by the desecuritization – understood as the unmaking of security – of immigration and asylum. For while Michael Williams has rightly argued that the submission of security to the democratic commitments of argumentative rationality can avoid the radical *realpolitik* that follows from exceptional acts and a Schmittian appeal to necessity and survival (Williams 2003: 523), it would be a mistake to equate securitization to such exceptional decisions only. Securitization also takes place in less dramatic circumstances and, in the case of the EU, the normalization of immigration policies has strengthened, rather than weakened, the security perspective in two ways.

First, the institutionalization of internal security as a means of reconciling the Union with its citizens has turned security into one of the fundaments of the European project. Since Amsterdam, the EU has sought to integrate EU-citizens within the AFSJ by turning their fears and misgivings into a mode of governance where trust is manufactured not so much through reassuring practices (such as those found in the welfare state, for example, where vulnerability is administered through social provisions, education and labour market policies), but through the exclusionary practices of threat management. Paradoxically, however, the reassurance of EU-citizens by means of security policies does not just restore citizens' trust in the EU but also produces the very anxieties and fears it responds to. The fears and misgivings of EU-citizens are not just prior to security responses. As was shown in Chapter 2, discourses of danger create security as well as insecurity, trust as well as fear.

Responding to fears and misgivings about immigration often involves an evaluation and assessment of migrants as a threat, i.e. as something to be feared. The public anxieties that internal security measures seeks to cure are thus also the product of security discourses through which immigrants are rendered as the 'illegal', '*bogus*' or 'criminal' other who is claimed to abuse or deny the fundamental right to freedom and free movement. As a result, the work of securing a community must constantly secure itself anew, as reassuring practices may generate new insecurities. Hence, from a political perspective the management of fear and misgivings through security practices is not necessarily a strategy for success. Paradoxically, as was also shown in the discussion of the security dilemma in Chapter 2, security practices continuously raise the bar of security to the point where security practices may radicalize relationships to immigrants and asylum-seekers without necessarily providing the promised reassurance. As Huysmans argues:

> The security spectacle is politically tricky. Evoking emergencies and dangers may simultaneously generate a need to control the fears by reassuring the members of the political community that one has the capacity to control the emergency. The latter can undermine governmental legitimacy because a continuation of insecurity may be interpreted as a sign of the incapacity of the government or the political class in general to manage the security problem (Huysmans 2006: 60).

Indeed, security does not mark the absence of threats but signifies a situation where one is confronted with a threat and some measure taken in response (Wæver 1995: 56).[10] Thus, security practices cannot itself provide a way out of the threat-defence sequence, as the goal of ever more security will spiral ever more insecurity. Indeed, without an understanding of the dialectics of security and insecurity, trust and fear it would not be possible to make sense of the paradox that 'despite more intensive attempts to control external borders, the problem of illegal entry is in many ways far more of a popular concern in many EU countries than it was in the first half of the 1990s, before EU and Schengen cooperation had really gained momentum' (Boswell 2003a: 102).

Second, while the normalization of security policies on immigration could have been expected to be more vulnerable to alternative validity claims put forward in counter discourses, the security discourse of the AFSJ has succeeded to neutralize and subsume alternative discourses and mobilizations under the security logic. First of all, the existence of alternative discourses to the dominant security frame does not necessarily undermine or challenge the dominant security discourse. To take part in the political struggle over the meaning of immigration, these discourses have to engage with the existing dominant discourse and the arguments put forwards there. Thus, counter discourses stressing that undocumented immigrants are not necessarily *bogus* or criminal; that the actual inflow of immigrants has been much lower than predicted in threat-scenarios; that the number of asylum-seekers is unconnected to the introduction of the internal market; and that current asylum-seeker application rates today are as low as in 1985 (see e.g., The European Council for Refugees and Exiles, The European Network Against Racism et al. 1999; UNCHR 2003) carry little weight in a security discourse that is not constructed around the measurement, evaluation and management of immigration in numbers but in terms of the fears and anxieties of EU-citizens. Hence, to challenge or resist the current security frame it is not enough to point out that the inflow of immigrants has decreased; one should also challenge the notion that security policy and threat management are crucial elements in bringing the Union closer to its citizens – for instance, by pointing out that security always also produces more insecurity and that the naming of threats to EU-citizens also may increase doubt about the Union's capacity to effectively manage these threats.

However, even when alternative discourses try to connect to the existing discourse, the knowledge of security professionals about how best to deal with threats will often prevent these discourses from penetrating the institutions of decision-making. Moreover, in the (few) cases where alternative forms of knowledge have been successfully mobilized, internal security officials have effectively subsumed these under the dominant discourse. Take for instance the introduction of a foreign affairs element in the management of immigration. The inclusion of foreign policy objectives in the management of immigration has been welcomed by NGOs concerned with the rights of immigrants and refugees because it would, in their view, shift the focus from the immigrant to the root causes of migration (The European Council for Refugees and Exiles, The European Network Against Racism et al. 1999). Also academics have pointed out that a more comprehensive approach to immigration would not just contribute to an improvement in the living conditions of potential immigrants in countries of destination but would also decrease the need for control measures (Niessen 1999; Boswell 2003b; Loescher and Milner 2003).

Yet, viewed in light of the more general objective of the development and maintenance of the AFSJ the difference between justice and home affairs objectives and foreign policy objectives appears less contradictory as is assumed by these actors. For regardless of whether the objective is 'to keep migrants and refugees out' (justice and home affairs) or 'to reduce the need to move' (foreign policy), both discourses share the same base-line assumption that migratory movement should be limited. For instance, the terms of references of the HLWG specify that it should focus on 'the most important countries of origin and transit of asylum seekers and migrants' (Coreper 1999). This shows that foreign affairs instruments and development objectives are made subordinate to the management of immigration and asylum flows. Although foreign policy may seek to improve living conditions in countries of destination under the banner of 'root causes', the dangerousness inscribed to migrant flows subverts and permeates these discourses. While foreign policy discourses regard the population of third countries as victims, their expert knowledge on how to improve the living conditions by targeting root causes is usurped by a politics of security, which operates on the basis that immigrants from countries that are judged to provide sufficient economic and political conditions can be *a priori* assumed to have moved without legitimate reasons. Or as the Austrian Strategy paper put it: 'In view of such interconnections [between security and foreign policy], crisis prevention, intervention and economic aid to poor States are not a substitute for restrictions on immigration and border controls, but both paths must be followed in parallel' (Austrian Presidency 1998: paragraph 57).

Besides the usurpation of the expert knowledge of foreign affairs, internal security professionals have also managed to seize upon supranational expert knowledge on the management of freedom. While the compensatory measures discourse already had given security experts a stake in the management of free movement, the objective of the AFSJ made the exercise of freedom even more dependent upon the management of threats insofar as security measures in the area of immigration are now seen as constitutive of freedom and the establishment of the AFSJ. With freedom defined in terms of security, supranational expertise in the shaping of freedom is without value unless it is complemented with security expertise. Hence, on both the discursive and institutional level, the Commission has adopted the more security-oriented discourse of justice and home affairs officials. The establishment of a DG-JHA within the European Commission, for instance, is symptomatic of the post-Amsterdam view that security is constitutive of freedom. Thus although tracing the division of decision-competences between the Commission and the member states can be significant for an understanding of the ways in which immigration is framed, the framing of freedom in terms of security has made the question of 'who speaks?' somewhat redundant: Both JHA officials as well as supranational actors concerned with free movement have accepted that freedom only obtains meaning when it is defined in the negative terms of a freedom from fear.

Conclusion

Within the European Studies literature, the intergovernmental conferences leading up to the signing of the Single European Act in 1986 and the Maastricht Treaty in 1992 are generally considered as the 'constitutional bargains', 'big bangs' or 'turning points' in the history of European integration. The Single European Act introduced the internal market and regulated the implementation of the so-called four freedoms (of goods, capital, services and persons), while the Maastricht Treaty founded the right to free movement as an important political step towards the establishment of an ever closer union between the peoples of Europe. By contrast, the Amsterdam Treaty is generally considered as much less of a political milestone. For example, Andrew Geddes argues that 'compared to the Maastricht Treaty, Amsterdam appears as an unambitious document' (Geddes 2000: 110). According to Moravcsik and Nicolaïdis, moreover, the 'Amsterdam Treaty ... is not likely to be remembered in the history of the European Union (EU), as the kind of watershed represented by its predecessors' (Moravcsik and Nicolaïdis 1999: 60).

Although these assessments of the Amsterdam Treaty may have some validity, they underestimate the political significance of the notion of the EU as an AFSJ. The introduction of the AFSJ has had an immediate political and normative bearing upon the EU-polity as a whole, since its aim is to integrate free individuals within the EU by means of threat management. As such, the AFSJ directly concerns central political and normative issues such as the rights of EU citizens, the relationship between EU-nationals with third country nationals as well as the way in which the EU relates to its external environment. Within the EU internal security management is not just a question of managing threats but a founding practice for the community that as it seeks to integrate individuals by means of governing their fears about excessive and improper forms of freedom.

5
Freedom, Mobility and Abjection: The Management of Immigration Risk in the AFSJ

Introduction: Framing freedom and security

The securing of freedom in the EU functions in ways that complicates and disturbs the dominant understanding of security as an exceptional practice bound-up with the sovereign protection of territoriality and centralized authority. Rather than functioning through juridical prohibition and drawing boundaries of life and death, security in the EU is directly related to the promotion of the mobility and circulation of populations, goods and services.

This chapter argues that this is not just the result of the interaction between bureaucratic and political practices in the European integration process. These practices need to be located in a wider context shaped by the preoccupation with freedom, circulation and risks central to (Foucauldian) advanced liberalism.

This liberal notion of security as a matter of ensuring circulation can be traced back to the art of governing that emerged in the 18th and 19th century. In his genealogical research on the state, Foucault pitches the liberal art of government as a historical response to two sets of doctrines, the doctrine of the *reason of state* and the *theory of police*, whose origins he dates back to the early 17th century (Foucault 2000a: 314). The doctrine of 'reason of state' – which today usually refers to the arbitrary exercise of state power – originally referred to a rationality of governing a state and its subjects with the aim of making the latter ever stronger (Foucault 2000a: 316). The theory of police is a correlative to this doctrine. Not restricted to its contemporary meaning of crime-fighting, police referred to a plethora of moral interventions aimed at making subjects more productive and active: 'As a form of rational intervention wielding political power over men, the role of the police is to supply them with a little extra life – and, by so doing, supply the state with a little extra strength' (Foucault 2000a: 319).

Although liberalism shares policing's concern with wealth, health and productivity of the population, its view on governing is considerably different than that put forward in doctrines of the reason of state. Most significantly, liberals depart from the view that order should be manufactured through continuous intervention in the affairs of society. Instead, they maintain that the state is limited in its capacity to know and control the social and economic affairs of its population (Foucault 2000b: 352). Security, wealth and productivity are not guaranteed through constant interventions but through ensuring the circulation already found within society. The aim of government is not to 'create order' but to 'guide disorder' (Agamben 2002).

While arguably less extreme than the Schmittian view of security as a force for creating order, liberal security performs its exclusionary function in more insidious ways. In fact, guiding disorder takes the form of targeted risk interventions. While the mobility of EU-citizens is promoted, the mobility of migrants, by effect of their risk class membership, is channelled through technologies of security which seek to render them increasingly immobile through preventing them from moving or, in case they move, by restricting and channelling their movement through technologies of risk management. Bigo has aptly described this shift as one from the *pan*optical to the *ban*optical, where specific groups are rendered suspect, 'simply by categorising them, anticipating profiles of risk from previous trends, and projecting them by generalization upon the potential behaviour of each individual pertaining to the risk category' (Bigo 2002: 81). As a result, the space of the border has been reconstituted around various axes, technologies and actors. No longer just a matter of patrolling the geographical border, the control of immigration flows has become a question of targeting risky spaces, risky populations and risky activities. Control is increasingly pro-active insofar as 'good' movement is separated from 'bad' movement already at the source. Security, then, manifests itself as a force of abjection excluding risky immigrants from trusted travellers.

This chapter will discuss the risk analysis, calculation, measurement and management of immigration risk more empirically. It argues that while targeted forms of interventions fit the liberal emphasis of limited rule, in practice, the idea of targeted governance may be self-perpetuating and self-reinforcing. Although risk management seeks to target specific groups, places and flows, the constant monitoring, control and correction of the targeted entity generates a continuous and self-renewing demand for more information and intelligence. Thus, the AFSJ has given rise to a multi-tiered 'Integrated Border Security Model' (EU Council 2002e: 9), which aims to prevent and stem the inflow of immigration at different stages through different technologies deployed by different actors.

Furthermore the management of immigration risk increasingly relies on the resources of private institutions and organizations. It will be argued that private actors have been reconstituted – sometimes involuntarily, sometimes more willingly – as risk managers through the commodification and marketization of immigration risk. Private actors, are summoned to partake in the management of immigration risk. Technologies such as carrier sanctions and visa-policy have enabled the commodification of immigration as a risk to be bought and sold on the market place as a result of which immigration management is increasingly a day-to-day responsibility for private institutions and organizations. Although the market-making of immigration risk entails a move away from a focus on public interventions, the private sector (for example, the insurance industry) has taken over the role of the government in monitoring whether private actors such as carriers live up to their obligations to manage immigration risk. Moreover, while privatization is generally viewed as a means of increasing policy effectiveness, risk management by private actors also transfers the authority to define threats and responses to the private sector with important consequences for the securitization of immigration.

Governing risk, targeting immigration

Immigration risk – the potential of undesirable movement into the EU by third country nationals – has increasingly become the principle according to which mobility is organized in the EU. By means of automated surveillance and verification technologies, specific categories of people are grouped together and singled out for risk-profiling regardless of whether or not they have committed a dangerous act. These technologies all operate upon the basis of mistrust where the possession of improper documents, short-term documents (which may entail the risk of visa-overstaying) and asylum-applications are all indexed as indicators of possible dangerous behaviour, whereas proper identification documents are taken as tokens of trust between the EU and its external environment. Broadly, risk technologies can be divided in three strands, each of which constitutes a separate filter or tier in the management of migration risk. Starting with pre-frontier measures and working our way up to the external EU-border, the most significant technologies are: (i) carrier sanctions, visa-policy and liaison officers (remote control); (ii) the proposal to introduce the camp as a buffer zone between EU-inside and EU-outside; and (iii) border management.

Remote control: Carrier sanctions, visas and liaison officers

The externalization of border management to third countries is a relatively recent but increasingly important node in the governance of mobility within and into the EU (van Munster and Sterkx 2005). Remote control takes place on the basis of the risk factor ascribed to certain places and people. Thus the comprehensive plan to combat illegal immigration and human trafficking speaks of '*targeted* measures in the countries of origin and transit' and, recognizing the need to organize information campaigns in the countries of destination, calls for '*concentrated* initiatives *targeted* at specific groups such as the unemployed, women or students' (EU Council 2002f: emphasis added). At the same time, however, it is recognized that raising awareness is unlikely to prevent the immigration risk: 'Does the public attention drawn by the European media to the serious accidents facing shipwreck victims on their journeys of despair affect the people attracted by the idea of immigration? By no means. Plans should be made to provide such people with specific information on this topic, but the impact would probably not be very great, given what successful migrants stand to gain' (EU Council 2003b).

In addition, therefore, the EU relies heavily on measures more directly related to control, surveillance and prevention. More specifically, the EU Schengen Catalogue on external borders control explicitly singles out the instruments of carrier sanctions, liaisons officers and the visa regime as the three core strategies in the control of immigration at a distance. In order to fully display the interconnectedness of these strategies, it is worth quoting the Schengen Catalogue at some length:

> The first measure required in terms of time and place is advice from liaison officers and document experts in third countries of origin or transit which are the source of the risks generated by illegal immigration ... Officials working abroad for the Schengen States' consular posts and carriers will be trained by specialists in order to detect document forgeries before actual travel has started ... In the second stage, a thorough inspection of the application documents submitted should be carried out by the Schengen States' consular representations when issuing visas ... The systematic implementation of EC/Schengen visa regulations should enable the phenomenon of illegal immigration to be effectively tackled at its roots. The importance of intensive consular cooperation should be stressed in that context. Carriers are also obliged ... to take all necessary means to ensure that third-country nationals carried by air, sea or land have the travel documents necessary for entry into the territory of the Schengen States (EU Council 2002e: 12–13).

By themselves, the idea to use carrier sanctions or identity-papers for the management of migration flows is hardly novel. The passport, for instance, has always been central in the management of population flows even though its function has changed significantly throughout history.[1] As for the concept of carrier sanctions, the 1905 UK Aliens Act already obliged ship captains to provide a list of alien passengers to state officials. Furthermore, various states already had integrated carrier sanction stipulations in their domestic immigration laws in place before the 1990 Schengen Implementing Agreement elaborated the notion of carrier sanctions on the European level.[2]

What is innovative about the European context, however, is the fact that carrier sanctions have been given an official status and high strategic significance in 'curbing migratory flows' and 'combating illegal immigration' (EU Council 2001). Where national control takes place largely at the geographical border, the EU has introduced a complex web of networked control where a transnational network of liaison officers assists consular officials and private carriers in the management of immigration. EU member states are sending and appointing liaison officers and document experts in third countries of origin and transit which are known as 'immigration hot spots'. Here, these specialists train airline security personnel in order to detect document forgeries before actual travel has started (EU Council 2002f: 17–18). Even the United Kingdom, a non-Schengen member, has acknowledged the importance of liaison officers within the context of EU cooperation: 'Our carriers' liability legislation places the onus on carriers to check that passengers are properly documented for travel to the UK. ALOs [Airline Liaison Officers] work in partnership with airlines abroad, offering advice on the acceptability of documents presented for travel. The Government is committed to playing a full part in the EU's action to improve the co-ordination of European ALO activities and enhance their training programmes' (Home Office 2002: 92–93).

Moreover, while the control over access to territory has traditionally been a prerogative of states, the introduction of the visa has somewhat weakened the state's monopoly to decide who has the right to enter and leave their territory. Since the ratification of the Maastricht Treaty the European Commission proposes the list of countries whose citizens require a visa for travel into the EU, which in turn recognizes that the EU has gained significant influence in regulating movement into EU-member states. While not without significance, the passport is no longer considered a sufficient identity mark for many third country nationals. In fact, most non-Western countries (including those known to produce political refugees) are listed as countries whose citizens require an additional visa for movement into and within the EU. Citizens belonging to countries on that list now also require a visa, which complements and supplants the identification function of the passport to which it is attached. Although it is impossible to obtain a visa without a legally valid passport, the visa is increasingly becoming an indicator of a person's identity.

Indeed, the visa has become constructed as an indispensable link in the management of undocumented immigration and has become part of the flanking measures designed to prevent the use of bogus or false identities (EU Council 1995). Indicative in this context is the decision to include pictures on visas, so that identity checks can be performed on the basis of the visa rather than the passport (EU Council 2002d). As the European Commission explains: 'One of the weaknesses of the system then in use was that neither the visa nor the residence permit, in sticker form, included any sort of photograph or other reliable means of identification. Consequently, it was decided that at the very minimum, it was urgent to provide for the incorporation into both documents of a photograph, meeting high security standards' (European Commission 2003a: 2). To further enhance the security standards of the uniform format for visas and travel documents in general, the EU has recently decided to also include biometric identifiers in the visa and the residence permit for third country nationals in order to establish a more reliable link between holder, passport and visa (EU Council 2002f: 12). Both the electronic photo and the biometric data of the visa applicant are to be stored in a European Visa Identification System (VIS), which is currently under development. The aim is to create a dual identification process based on secure documents and a database which contains details of visas applied for, issued and refused so that an integrated risk assessment of all visa applicants can take place:

> The main issues to be borne in mind when examining visa applications are: the security of the Contracting Parties and the fight against illegal immigration as well as other aspects relating to international relations ... The diplomatic mission or consular post shall assume full responsibility in assessing whether there is an *immigration risk*. The purpose of examining applications is to detect those applicants who are seeking to immigrate to the territory of the Contracting Parties and set themselves up there, using grounds such as tourism, studies, business or family visits as a pretext. Therefore, it is necessary to be particularly vigilant when dealing with '*risk categories*', in other words unemployed persons, and those with no regular income etc. If there is any doubt over the authenticity of the papers and supporting documents submitted, the diplomatic mission or consular post shall refrain from issuing a visa (EU Council 2002a: emphasis added).

Moreover, the visa regime enables a much more selective sorting and targeting of risky categories than the passport allowed for. Compared to the passport, the visa is able to prevent and channel movement in a much more detailed way through the specification of time limits and the modalities of movement. Indeed, to date the EU distinguishes between: (i) an airport transit visa; (ii) a transit visa; (iii) a travel visa; (iv) a multiple entry visa; (v) a group visa; (vi) a long-stay visa; and (vii) a visa with limited territorial validity – all of which have different ramifications for the conduct of mobility within and into EU territory.

A visa, then, is only issued when the visa application, travel documents and supporting documents are approved. As Bigo and Guild (2004) have shown, the issuing of a visa therewith also includes a verification of an applicant's good faith. For whereas a passport is obtained by birth, the visa is a token of trust handed out only to those who deserve it, that is, those who are considered not to constitute an 'immigration risk'. But since the visa is an individual document of trust, there remains a permanent need to police and control those that are not in the possession of such a token of trust, but nevertheless decide to migrate.

Between inside and outside: Building buffer zones

The second technology to manage immigration flows into the EU that I would briefly like to discuss is the camp. Like carrier sanctions and identity-papers, the camp is not a new technology in the management of refugee populations. Since World War II, the refugee camp has been viewed as an efficient means of distributing aid and managing displacement (Hyndman 2000). But the camp also had a more political function. It was the space where refugees were categorized and managed with the purpose of turning them into individuals well-suited for resettlement in other states. In this view, the camp operated in similar ways to the factory, asylum, barracks, school and prison. As Lippert argues, 'it was not just food, water, and medical aid that was dispensed through the camp; it was discipline' (Lippert 1999: 309). The overall objective of the refugee camp was to train and prepare individuals for a life outside this institution. Concomitantly, camp inhabitants were expected to remain in the camp for as short a period of time as possible, because – not unlike the welfare recipient in Western states – their dependence on food, water and other forms of aid was considered to turn them into dependent, unproductive individuals ill-suited and ill-prepared for resettlement.[3]

Within the context of the EU, the camp has reemerged first and foremost as a tool for guiding, steering and managing immigration flows. The objective is not disciplinary; rather, the primary function of these camps seems to be the prevention of spontaneous arrivals of asylum-seekers in the EU. Following the June 2003 Thessaloniki European Council which invited the Commission 'to explore all parameters in order to ensure more orderly and managed entry in the EU of persons in need of international protection' (European Council 2003), the Commission has presented a communication in which it proposes that asylum claims should be processed outside EU-territory (European Commission 2004). As a space where good movement can be separated from bad movement, the camps enables certain groups to be channelled into processing, while other groups – most likely undocumented immigrants – can be refused access to the EU before their claims are considered. As such, the objective of the camp is comparable to that of the visa regime and other forms of control that seek to separate desirable forms of movement from undesirable ones. In cases where these refugees cannot be returned to their country of destination, they run the risk of indefinite detainment within these camps.

The idea to process immigrants in camps specifically designed for that purpose was launched by the United Kingdom under the title of 'a new vision of refugees'. This plan calls for the establishment of a global network of 'safe havens' which were defined as 'particular camps whose prime purpose is to provide a place of safety and process claims' (Home Office 2003: 10). According to the plan, asylum-seekers need not travel to the EU but should directly go to one of the camps where they could lodge their asylum claims. In addition, the plan suggests that any asylum-seeker arriving in the UK or elsewhere in the EU would be relocated to one of these safe havens. In a paper attached to a letter to the Greek Presidency during the first half of 2003, UK Prime Minister Tony Blair called for the improved regional management of migration flows and launched the notion of 'transit processing centres' (Blair 2003).

Rather than a temporary place for the disciplining of refugees, 'regional protection zones' and 'transit processing centres' just outside the EU territory function more like buffer-zones for the control and monitoring of migration flows. The re-allocation of all immigrants to process centres, moreover, is also meant to have a deterring effect on undocumented immigrants trying to enter EU-territory (The Observer 2003). In contrast to the functioning of the refugee camp as a place of discipline, the idea of transit processing centres would institutionalize the camp as a place of exclusion, where undocumented or improperly documented immigrants can be refused entry without a prior evaluation of their reasons for moving.[4] The notion of the camp as a buffer zone between the EU (inside) and its external environment (outside) can be seen as a logical extension of both the Dublin Convention principle of country of first asylum and the readmission agreements concluded between the EU and third countries. But the camp also goes beyond readmission and the country of first asylum principle. The latter target immigrants upon arrival and can therefore be described as being largely reactive in nature. The camp, however, targets immigrants already before arrival and is therefore best described as a pro-active form of 'buffering'.

While the June 2004 Commission communication claims that regional process centres are beneficial for immigrants as 'there would be no need for those in need of protection to pay traffickers thousands of Euros for a dangerous and illegal journey to the EU' (European Commission 2004: 6; see also European Commission 2003b), the overall objective seems to be to manage the immigration risk. First of all, the fact that immigrants have to turn to human traffickers is to a large degree the result of EU measures that make it increasingly difficult for asylum-seekers to enter the EU in a more conventional way. If the objective is to prevent human trafficking, it is thus very unlikely that the introduction of camps will contribute in any significant way to this objective. It is highly unlikely that immigrants that make use of the services of human traffickers will be deemed amenable for refugee status, which in turn means that these immigrants would have no reason to make use of transit processing centres. Rather than the right to seek protection, then, the European Commission seems concerned more with establishing the conditions for decisions about access on the basis of the socio-economic and security needs of the state rather than those of refugees:

> [I]n general, the legal, orderly and managed entry to the EU would allow the Member States to anticipate the arrival of the persons determined to be in need of international protection. This advance notice could bring a number of advantages in terms of planning: for housing and the inevitable financial impact. The setting up of tailor made integration programmes for specific categories of refugees would also be much easier devised if a country knew in advance who was arriving on its territory to stay. Resettling and allowing physical access to the territory of the EU of persons whose identity and history has been screened in advance would also be preferable from a security perspective (European Commission 2004: 6–7).

One of the central functions of the camp, then, is to carry out 'pre-arrival security checks' (European Commission 2004: 7) on immigrants whose 'dangerousness' has not been determined already at the root by means of visa-application assessments or other control procedures. Together with pre-frontier control measures such as carrier, sanctions, visa policy and liaison officers the creation of buffer zones in the form of transit process centres have a deep impact upon the space of the border and the geographical notion of border control.

Towards knowledge-based border management

Within Schengen the airport and other border sites play an important role in the management of illegal immigration. Now part of the Union's Schengen *acquis*, the Schengen Executive Committee argued in 1994 that:

> Airports play a key role in the Schengen system: firstly, they are of considerable importance as an access point for an ever-increasing number of travellers and consequently also for illegal immigrants; secondly, they serve as both internal and external borders and therefore constitute a specific sector facing a series of specific problems (Schengen 1994).

The functioning of borders as sites of control and surveillance is not new, however. Airports in particular have traditionally deployed a great assortment of technologies such as CCTV, passports, visas, baggage control, boarding passes and identity cards to govern and monitor the conduct of mobility (Lisle 2003: 18). In fact, borders have always performed a double function. On the one hand, they have enabled the conduct of freedom by making it possible for travellers to cross borders; on the other hand, borders have also played an important role in the surveillance and control of populations with the aim of protecting the national population from outside threats. Nevertheless, Schengen cooperation has fundamentally changed the essence of the geopolitical border in the EU (Walters 2002). But where Walters sees this change as a shift from the control of territory (geopolitics) to the control of life (biopolitics), this change is perhaps itself part of the broader shift from the Schmittian rationality to a more liberal logic that operates in a more targeted sense on the basis of informational codes. Thus while Schengen does not completely do away with material control and gateways, it nonetheless signifies a departure from the idea of the border as enclosing a territory that needs to be protected against outside threats. Rather Schengen calls for knowledge-based border control, where borders are the final filter in the integrated management of immigration risk.

Border crossing points have become an important node in the management of European security and mobility and the physical space of the airport, seaport and other official entry points have been redesigned and reorganized according to the multi-tiered approach to migration management. Thus the Schengen Catalogue calls for an interactive, management of borders based on risk knowledge and risk communication: '[V]arious methodologies should be applied at the borders. Terms such as risk analysis, intelligence, data-flow management, situational awareness, reaction capability and information exchange with other Schengen States can be used when evaluating and developing these methods' (EU Council 2002e: 16). As a result, border controls no longer predominantly function as the site of extensive pass controls and personal checks that bring into play the national sovereignty of the state. In fact, control increasingly takes place before departure (by consulates, carriers, liaison officers or, perhaps in the near future, by professionals employed in offshore process centres), while border management has become a question of verifying the previously issued identity and travel documents on the basis of risk information stored in databases and the risk knowledge that circulates between different organizations.

This new function of verification, in turn, is supported and made possible by administrative and technological systems. For instance, Schengen requires airports and seaports to be designed so that the flow of third country nationals can be separated from intra-EU travel (EU Council 2002e: 25–26). This architectural redesign has enabled security verification procedures to target more directly the identity of persons originating from outside the EU. Second, new control boxes have been introduced where security officials can check identity documents against the data stored in the SIS. If in doubt about the authenticity of documentation, border guards are assisted by the so-called Schengen documentation centre, which has specialized in the technological verification of identity documents (e.g., boarding passes, travel tickets, visas and passports).

Most significantly, however, is the fact that trust or mistrust in the individual is in the process of being replaced by trust in risk technologies aimed at the identification and authorization of potentially dangerous groups. On top of the patrolling of territorial borders, border control has very much become about the collection and dispersion of knowledge on risky flows of mobility. Thus the Deputy Chief Superintendent of the Danish Border Police, originally responsible for physical border control, confirms that his task has increasingly moved towards the collection and dissemination of risk knowledge on immigration. As he defines his current job:

> Every month I go and find out what the travel trend is, on which weekdays they come, and things like that, which I then send out. On top of that, I send out an 'illegal travel trend' every Friday, where I take information from various national and international intelligence services and send them to all colleagues in the airport and I also send a copy to the three major companies operating in the airport. For often it concerns things, which they can prevent from their departure destinations before [immigrants] get here ... I put [the information] together in a monthly overview about what happened; how many asylum-seekers – almost categorise them. Can we see when asylum-seekers come? Which flights are they on? And things like that, so that one can perhaps make flight companies look more specifically into certain flight departures (Interview, 24 November 2004).

While this is perhaps most advanced in the case of air borders, due to the organized nature of air travel and the enclosed space of airports making them particularly suited to the application of high-tech control measures, the shift towards integrated risk management is also discernible for land and maritime borders (EU Council 2003b). Here, too, border control increasingly takes the form of managing abstract knowledge about the risk of certain flows which requires that border officials are in constant contact with liaison officers, foreign colleagues, private carriers and risk information centres such as the Air Borders Centre in Rome, the Centre for Land Borders in Berlin, Maritime Borders Centres in Madrid and Piraeus, COLPOFOR (Cooperation of European Railway Police and Security Services) and the Risk Analysis Centre in Helsinki (see EU Council 2003c; EU Council 2003d; EU Council 2003a). In 2004, these diffuse centres were integrated in Frontex to improve information coordination and dissemination efforts. Based in Warsaw, Frontex is an intelligence driven EU agency with the task to coordinate the operational cooperation between Member States in the field of border security (EU Council 2004).

Working as a form of informational power, risk surveillance is moving away from concrete bodies and focuses instead upon flows of data as the stand-ins for real bodies. The best-known example is the SIS, which has become an important instrument in the stemming of migration flows. While the SIS is seen mainly as an instrument against organized crime (hence its inclusion in the third pillar; see Chapter 3), 89% of the entries in the SIS are on undocumented migrants, which comes down to a total of 778,886 records related to 'illegal aliens' (Statewatch 2005).[5] The profiling of undocumented immigrants through SIS is further reinforced by the introduction of Eurodac and the planned introduction of the VIS, which store images and biometric data (fingerprints) of asylum-seekers, undocumented immigrants and visa applicants. These databases go a step further than the SIS. Whereas the latter only allows data to be recorded in relation to criminal matters (illegality is considered a serious crime in countries such as Germany and France but not in Belgium and Denmark), the only criterion for having fingerprints recorded in Eurodac and VIS is the fact that an individual has applied for asylum or for a visa. With the implementation of the Eurodac-database and the plans for a VIS, undocumented immigrants, asylum-seekers and immigrants more generally will thus be subjected to categorical suspicion and made amenable to targeted practices of risk management.

The border, then, is becoming a node in a transnational risk communication system where border police has joined up with other institutions in the search for perfect risk knowledge. For instance, the data used by the border police is also increasingly coupled to consumer data gathered by private carriers. For commercial purposes, private carriers often store information related to the purchase of a ticket. However, as identification and verification increases the importance of risk profiling, consumer data has become increasingly relevant for security officials in their attempt to assess the levels of dangerousness of mobile flows. As the Deputy Chief Superintendent of the Danish Border Police claims with regard to the targeting of Chinese travellers:

> [E]very time you hear the word 'Chinese', you assume something is suspect about them ... In Denmark we have 13 flights from China

> a week, so we go through the passenger lists to see if some tickets are bought together. Can we see any groups, or any other things we can use for profiling? How are tickets bought – are they paid in cash or are they paid for 3 weeks in advance? We say that if something is paid in cash, it could be human smuggling or something [because] large firms do not use cash today (Interview, 24 November 2004).

Information concerning the payment of a ticket, the amount of tickets bought and under which names, the routes, transits and different companies involved, the historical record of a consumer – in principle, everything can be recoded as signs of the risk-level of people, activities and places.

The commodification of immigration risk

The management of immigration risk according to liberal rationality has not just reshaped bureaucratic practices of security. It has also transformed the role of private actors in the routine management of immigration risk. If understood as sovereign, exceptional practices, security is implicitly understood as a task for public actors. After all, only the state can recourse to extraordinary security measures that bypass the normal rules of society. Within the liberal logic of security as a means of managing mobility, immigration management is constituted as a day-to-day responsibility not only for public but also for private institutions and organizations.

Arguably, the threat of carrier sanctions has been the most direct mode through which the responsibility for immigration control has been delegated to the private sector. Through the threat of carrier sanctions, the identity and function of private companies without a stake in security management are recoded as those responsible for the management of migration risk. Faced with the high economic costs of carrier sanctions, private carriers have thus started to take additional measures to ensure that third country nationals are in possession of valid travel documents upon entering the Schengen territory. These measures consist of tightened security and control checks at departure and sometimes arrival, the establishment of contacts with police authorities and liaison officers, risk profiling on the basis of consumer data and the training of personnel in document identification. Moreover, some airlines have also started to hire personnel with a background as security professionals. For instance, Air France's security department is now led by a former official from the Ministry of the Interior with previous work experience in the areas of border control and terrorism (Guiraudon 2001: 54).

The carrier sanctions regime, in turn, is complemented by benchmarking and performance based evaluation schemes, which offer carriers partial or full relief from sanctions if they agree to fulfil certain conditions regarding immigration control. Typical for the advanced liberal way of governing, benchmarking, the setting of performance and 'best practice' marks seek to shape the conditions under which private actor start governing themselves in the most optimal sense. Their aim is to create and subsume the specialized expertise of risk management to formal calculative standards that ensure efficiency, quality and effectiveness measured in terms of productivity. As the Facilitation Manager of British Airways, James Forster, explains: 'Once the [best practice] status is achieved, the carrier will not be fined for passengers arriving from that airport without any documents' (Forster 2002: 28).

Yet, the involvement of private carriers in the management of migration risk has not just been encouraged with the 'stick' of carrier sanctions and benchmarking. For carriers, for instance, it can also be economically rewarding to become actively involved in the management of immigration risk. The consular instructions on how to issue a visa states that all applicants should be interviewed in order to assess whether or not the person involved constitutes an immigration risk. The amount of work involved with the issuing of visa has overburdened many consulates as every individual applicant needs to be interviewed to verify the objectives of the journey. To relieve consulates from this time consuming task, the EU has decided that these interviews may be delegated to private parties such as travel agencies and carriers. Originally, the scope for private involvement was limited to group travel only (EU Council 2002a: 5), but a Council Decision on the adaptation of the common consular instructions has widened the scope of private involvement beyond group travel:

> It is both common and useful, particularly in countries with a large surface area, for private administrative agencies, travel agencies, and tour operators and their retailers to act as authorized intermediaries of the applicant ... [T]he degree of solvency and reliability

> expected of them will, in principle, be directly proportional to their degree of involvement in the overall planning of the journey, accommodation, medical and travel insurance, and their responsibility for the client's return to the country of origin (EU Council 2002b: , article 2)

Perceptively, Elspeth Guild (2004) has shown that being recognized and authorized as a 'reputable and trustworthy body [that] is able to vouch for the good faith of those persons concerned' (EU Council 2002a: 5) comes with important economic benefits for private carriers and travel agencies. For them, it means that fewer seats will remain empty as a result of persons not having been able to obtain a visa in time. This certainty allows them to operate with lower costs than competitors that have not been granted the trust status. To this it could be added that if airline companies manage to fill carrier seats with passengers with pre-approved documents, this will also reduce their vulnerability to fines and sanctions payable for improperly documented travellers. Simultaneously, it is also likely to increase the performance status of carriers, which may release them from paying fines in the cases where people of 'ill faith' have actually managed to board their vessels.

Thus, while the Council Decision explicitly states that the 'purpose of defining the conditions for cooperation with travel agencies is not to inhibit free competition' (EU Council 2002b), a refusal to cooperate (e.g., by refusing to be involved in what companies may believe to be a public task or by refusing to treat their clients as suspects), they are likely to suffer significant operation costs, resulting in a worse market position than competitors that have accepted their responsibility in the management of migration flows into the EU. Confronted with a series of interwoven economic incentives, carriers are pushed, without direct public interventions, to ensure that policies are in line with EU desires and objectives.

Obviously, the privatization of immigration control through carrier sanctions has not gone unnoticed in the literature on immigration control (Lahav 1998; Miles 1999; Guiraudon 2000; Verstraete 2001). For instance, Guiraudon has identified privatization as a means of 'venue shopping' by which means states seek to circumvent national and international legal constraints on the control of immigrants (Guiraudon 2000; Guiraudon and Lahav 2000; Guiraudon 2001).

Lahav, in turn, has conceptualized privatization as an instance of state expansion, whereby the state seeks to obtain the state objective of immigration control through the creation of dense regulatory webs between public and private actors (Lahav 1998). Whether or not privatization is indeed an explicit attempt to skirt legal obligations, this has very much been the outcome in practice. For while the 2001 EU directive on carrier sanctions stipulates that the directive 'is without prejudice to the obligations resulting from the Geneva Convention relating to the Status of Refugees of 28 July 1951, as amended by the New York Protocol of 31 January 1967' (EU Council 2001), the devolution of immigration control has severely limited the possibilities of immigrants to seek asylum. For example, James Forster, the Facilitation Manager of British Airways, states that airlines confronted with the real possibility of carrier sanctions have actually denied persons the opportunity to claim asylum by preventing them from flying:

> We understand that, since 1987, no fewer than 400 passengers, who boarded British Airways flights with apparently correct travel documentation and yet arrived in the UK without valid documents, have been granted refugee status in the UK ... As a direct result of carriers' liability legislation, British Airways and other carriers have refused carriage to thousands of passengers. How many of these would have been granted refugee status had they reached the UK is unknown (Forster 2002: 27).[6]

Private companies which detect undocumented migrants on board are first and foremost interested in determining and verifying their country of origin so that repatriation efforts can be undertaken before the sanctions regime begins to apply. Confronted with the burden of carrier sanctions, carriers are pushed to view prevention and repatriation in terms of loss prevention, while undocumented immigrants are constructed as economic operation costs. As a result, companies have no incentive (nor the means) to examine the legal rightfulness of asylum claims and tend to focus upon the control and repatriation of immigration. Take for instance the case of Robmarine Shipping Consultants (RSC), a UK-based all-round shipping assistance company which assists shipping companies in the repatriation of undocumented immigrants found on board of their vessels. Because undocumented immigrants are an economic risk, it is imperative for companies that find themselves confronted with stowaways to repatriate them as quickly as possible and before the sanctions regime starts to apply. To help companies with verifying the identity of stowaways, RSC argues that successful repatriation of a stowaway largely depends on the procurement of an emergency travel document, which in turn depends upon acquiring high quality photographs and statements for use by embassies and consuls. To this end, RSC has provided a questionnaire containing 68 questions that can help determining the stowaway's country of origin or transit. Because none of the 68 questions is related to the motives stowaways may have had for leaving their country, the possibility to seek asylum is significantly reduced and made subordinate to the economic objective of repatriation.[7]

While the writings on the privatization of immigration control have contributed significantly to our understanding of the ways in which immigration control functions and the effects it has on the human rights regime, two objections can be raised against the explanations for why immigration control has been privatized. The first one concerns the generally shared assumption that the objective of carrier sanctions is to make immigration control more effective and efficient. The second one follows from this and concerns the statement that privatization strengthens rather than weakens the state and/or public authority.

Privatization and the argument of policy effectiveness

Generally, the privatization of immigration control by means of carrier sanctions is justified as a means of policy effectiveness, whereby public actors can attain goals they are unable to reach themselves (Lahav 1998; Guiraudon 2001). While the argument of policy effectiveness no doubt underpins many decisions on privatization, it is not totally convincing in the case of carrier sanctions and immigration control. For if policy effectiveness is the goal, it is somewhat unclear why railways, which are generally in the hands of the public rather than the private sector, have been exempted from the regime of carrier sanctions.

Carrier sanctions, then, are not just about policy effectiveness; they are also a way of engaging the private sector in the management of migration risk. They illustrate the advanced liberal motto of 'governing without governing society', i.e. the view that governing is about self-government rather than direct public intervention. This ideal has been promoted, most notably, by what could be referred to as the 'marketization of immigration risk', i.e. the inscription of undocumented immigration as a business risk or 'damage' against which insurance is possible. Marketization can be defined as an advanced liberal means of steering private actors through economic incentives (carrier sanctions) that create conditions for the purchase and selling of security via the market place.

The involvement of insurance companies is interesting not only because it serves as an example of how private actors, through the selling and buying of the economic risk of stowaways on the market place, can earn money in the business of immigration control. It is also interesting because it turns insurance into a form of security governance beyond the state. That is, private insurance companies have started taking over the governing and monitoring role of public authorities by enforcing preventive security requirements upon the carriers they insure.[8] For instance, Club P&I, a specialized insurance company in the shipping industry, regularly reminds shipping companies in its StopLoss Bulletin 'of the need for great vigilance to prevent stowaways gaining access to any part of their vessels before leaving port, especially in those areas of the world where stowaways are known to be a serious potential problem' (The London P&I Club 2004: 2). In association with Videotel Marine International, P&I Club has also designed a training video and booklet ('Coping with Stowaways') to instruct officers and crew on the problems caused by stowaways, including advice on how to prevent stowaways from getting aboard ships and the steps to be taken if stowaways are discovered.[9]

Through the marketization of immigration risk, then, insurance companies rule the insured by fostering vigilance and precaution in an attempt to limit the frequency of loss. This points to an important contradiction in the rationality of advanced liberalism. While it promises less governance, the 'liberal fear of governing too much is not so much a fear that the population is governed too much but that the state is doing too much of the governing' (Dean 2002: 42). It is not a fear of regulation *per se*; the marketization of immigration risk has brought about a dense web of regulatory relations, where private insurance companies have assumed the governing role by making sure that the insured manage risks in the most optimal sense.

Privatization and the authority to construct security

The argument that privatization serves to increase policy effectiveness is closely related to the paradox that privatization strengthens rather than weakens the state. Generally, the involvement of the private sector is explained as a process of state expansion whereby the state extends control by means of privatization (Lahav 1998). However, a closer look reveals that this paradox is a false one for at least two reasons. The first is that privatization entails that private actors may increasingly define threats through the collection, analysis and boxing of information about immigration risk. The second is that the privatization and marketization of immigration risk results in self-perpetuating market mechanisms that increase the demand for security and which cannot be controlled by the state or any other public authority (Leander 2005b). Left to the private sector, the governance of immigration risk has important consequences for the securitization of immigration.

As regards the power to set the security agenda, private actors have begun to engage themselves in the business of risk communication and categorization. Although it is still the case that public clearing houses such as CIREA, CIREFI and Frontex collect and disperse most of the information on immigration risk, private actors too have started to group and collect risk information on undocumented immigration. They have started doing so not because they have been hired to provide the information on immigration risk; rather, the commodification of immigration risk has given the carriers industry and their insurers an economic incentive to invest in the gathering and dispersion of risk information. To return to the example of RSC, this company has started to produce data on stowaways, which can be freely accessed on the Internet. Striving to provide their 'clients with a service that is realistic yet challenging; practical yet innovative; sensible yet creative; sympathetic yet exciting', the more specific objective of the website on stowaways is to create a 'multimedia library of information that all users, claims handlers, correspondents and agents can investigate and benefit from.'[10] To date, the site provides detailed information on immigration 'problem nations' and immigration 'hot spots', while the website also gives computerized access to an 'extensive computerised stowaway database consisting of photographs, travel documents and fingerprints based on nine years of stowaway documentation and repatriation'.[11]

Although the risk analyses undertaken by RSC and others may well contribute to the objectives of public policy-making, it does not automatically follow that this also strengthens the public sector, as suggested by Guiraudon and Lahav. To the contrary, if private firms start to gather, group and disperse the information on undocumented migration flows, their analyses may increasingly come to inform public decisions on what is or is not a threat, where threats occur and where targeted interventions based on risk information should take place. As the RSC explains, the aim of accumulating accurate data is 'to provide governments with statistics that highlight the extent of the stowaway problem', no doubt, in the hope that governments will act on this information and re-allocate their risk interventions accordingly.[12] In such cases, the security agenda could increasingly come to mirror particular business interests as the public focus is redirected to those places where companies are suffering losses because of the risk of undocumented immigration.

The norms of what constitutes a threat is not just established by the collection, categorization and boxing of information. Norms about what constitutes good and bad behaviour are sometimes already incorporated in the technologies deployed. For instance, to get around the problem that someone has to keep a constant eye on CCTV camera images, new devices are appearing that can single out and zoom in on 'strange' behaviour. If, for example, someone starts running in an airport terminal, such a system will recognize this as anomalous behaviour. Similarly, the firm Land Instruments has developed a thermal device that can identify body temperature and fever. Used mainly in the context of the Sars epidemics, it has been suggested that the technology could also be used in the future to pinpoint terrorists or illegal immigrants, who may be sweating before departure (BBC 2003). In these cases, sweating and running are encoded as behavioural deviances that signal risk. Besides the question of whether these norms are in fact meaningful (is running in an airport really anomalous behaviour?), the important point is that these technologies articulate a certain power through their design. In an attempt to cut down human chance, they impact upon the routines of border guards whose perception of normality is shaped by the technologies available to them. These direct them to scrutinize certain aspects and activities of their target-population more energetically than others.

Second, the authority of the public sector is undermined because of independent market dynamics, which generate a constant supply (and hence demand) in technologies of risk management and risk communication. Under conditions of liberalism, security is not only a technique of governing dependent populations, but also a profitable industry. The control of immigration is not only a burden for the private sector but also a potentially lucrative enterprise, where money can be made in border control, detention, repatriation and the development of new security technologies, (de Stoop 1996; Verstraete 2001). Or as David Lyon eloquently puts it, 'places of high risk as danger are also places of high risk as economic adventure' (Lyon 2003: 47). On the immigration risk market, sellers of surveillance and other security technologies (biometric systems, detection devices, etc.) have to convince their potential buyers that they provide the best answer to the immigration risk. As their expertise is based on claims of technological competence and economic efficiency, they will often tend to stress the technico-managerial aspect of security (Leander 2005b). For instance, the Steria Group, the company in charge of implementing the biometric Eurodac system, claims that '[t]he identification system is exceptionally efficient and precise, with a capacity of about 500,000 comparisons per second and a precision rate of over 99,9%' (Steria 2003b). On the basis of these technological performance rates the 'European Commission was convinced that the Cogent AFIS system [Automatic Fingerprint Identification System], the proposed architecture and the hardware and the flexibility of the team was the answer to their 'pain'' (Steria 2003a).[13]

As such, the failure of risk management and risk technologies do not necessarily undermine the risk market; it is more likely that these failures will feed back into the technologically driven imperative to tame uncertainty and master the hazard of immigration. Because a clear picture of the threat is missing, it is difficult to determine when a threat has passed and surveillance can be terminated. Threats always remain potential, which justifies constant risk awareness. Once one is locked into discussions of immigration along the technical lines of argumentation, the failure to prevent immigrants entering EU-territory may become a driving-factor for more advanced forms of risk management in order to decrease the likelihood of such events occurring in the future.

In this view, uncertainty regarding the usefulness of these technologies widens the market for immigration risk. It gives sellers the opportunity to shape their clients' understanding of the threat as well as the most adequate responses to it. For instance, the decision to use fingerprints rather than iris-scanning (even though the latter is deemed more reliable than fingerprinting) as the biometric identifier for Eurodac seems based on the belief that fingerprint technology will provide the best conditions for interoperability and innovation (European Commission 2003a).[14]

However, it is important to note that the effectiveness of these technologies to alleviate the 'pain' of undocumented immigration remains uncertain. Nobody really knows the precise extent of undocumented immigration which, by its very nature, escapes measurement and calculation. It is unknown how effective technological solutions are in managing the immigration risk, simply because it is unclear how large a percentage of the total number of undocumented immigrants they actually manage to apprehend. Moreover, border control, no matter how technologically advanced, is highly unlikely to be effective in the management of immigration, which is a complex phenomenon that defies easy technological solutions. To discuss immigration mainly in the technico-managerial terms of the sellers of risk technologies precludes public debate on the political, economic and social context of immigration and political action. Indeed, the marketization and commodification of immigration as a risk to be bought and sold on the market place contributes to the securitization of immigration because it creates (and not just responds to) the demand for the services they offer (see also Leander 2005a).

Conclusion: Risk and the contradictions of liberalism

This chapter has discussed the ways in which security in the EU expresses and has been transformed by the advanced liberal view of 'governing without governing society'. Rather than a sovereign politics of exception, security has taken the form of knowledge-driven risk interventions targeted at 'risky places' (borders, third countries), 'risky activities' (unauthorized movement) and 'risky categories' (asylum-seekers, undocumented immigrants). Whereas traditionally the space of governance has been conceived in terms of a relation between a national population and national territory defined by the geographical border, security governance in the EU has been first and foremost oriented towards the problem of connecting and reconstructing the EU as a zone of mobility. In this image of the AFSJ, targeted forms of risk management are about ruling the interstices, and stitching the holes and breaches in the security system. For as the comprehensive plan on illegal immigration and human trafficking argues: 'The common security system is only as strong as its weakest point ... Illegal immigrants take advantage of gaps at border controls and other deficiencies in control measures' (EU Council 2002f).

The advanced liberal rationality of managing insecurity, it was argued, gave rise to two major contradictions. First, while targeted governance is intended as a limited way of intervening in the affairs of people, the management of immigration has led to an insatiable demand for risk information. Risk management presupposes total information awareness at all time and all places. As the Schengen Catalogue puts it: 'Reliable estimates concerning border checks and surveillance measures should be based, among other things, on *complete* knowledge of regional and local circumstances ... Valid and reliable data should form part of a *permanent* evaluation which could be shared by other Schengen States' (EU Council 16 2002e, emphasis added). Heidegger has nicely captured the essence of what could be referred to as the information-governance paradox:

> The work for the securing of life ... must constantly secure itself anew. The guiding word for this fundamental attitude of contemporary existence speaks: Information ... In the first place, information means the reporting that instructs modern men, as quickly and as comprehensively as possible, as clearly and completely as possible, about the securing of his needs, their requirement and their provision ... However, while information in-forms, that is, reports, at the same time it forms, that is, it organizes and directs (cited in Ericson and Haggerty 1997: 85–86).

In the context of the EU, the quest for more accurate and more detailed information has led to a multiplication of controls and surveillance. Although the border in many ways still is a spectacle of surveillance, effectual control often takes place before travellers arrive at the border, while the border itself is increasingly an important nodal point in transnational networks of control that consist of public and private actors. Proposals to create buffer zones between inside and outside (i.e. processing centres and regional protection zones) can be seen as a further indication of the desire to categorize populations in terms of the potential harm they pose. Although advanced liberalism presents itself as a limited form of rule, immigration management in the EU thus hardly contributes to its ideal of governing less.

The second contradiction of the advanced liberal project is that governance is not just encouraged by the public search for ever-better information but also by private actors who are increasingly taking over tasks related to immigration management. As the commodification and marketization of immigration risk extended the regulation of immigration risk to the private sector, private actors such as insurers who provide coverage against the risk of undocumented immigration have taken over the role traditionally performed by the public sector. Instead of public intervention, there now exists a dense web of contractual obligations that monitor hierarchical relations in the private sphere.[15]

Moreover, the technico-managerial practices of risk management tend to be self-propelling as a result of independent market dynamics by means of which the supply of technical security solutions creates the demand for these products and, hence, for more governance. Risk management tends to encourage a technical debate and gives the impression the complex socio-economic problems can be solved by 'easy' technological solutions. This technico-managerial framing precludes a more fundamental process of public deliberation on how to mediate the relationship between self and other. For what may seem a question of managerial question of abject populations is in the end also a political question of who is allowed access to the social fabric of society and how society should be structured (Huysmans 1998: 570). To speak of migration in terms of risk is also to articulate a particular politics of belonging. And the distribution of trust and fear has a fundamental impact upon how freedom is distributed. The EU as an AFSJ has been made visible and governable through the deployment of deterritorialized, networked risk technologies. Through these forms of risk interventions, the EU-order is increasingly imagined and governed as a space of unease where individuals are integrated through their concerns and worries about undocumented immigrants and other unwanted forms of mobility. The Union's emphasis on freedom *qua* mobility, then, leads to a form of 'negative solidarity', which creates a community whose only commonality is that of risk. In this community, the prevention of 'bads' rather than the production of goods' is the organizing principle through which the EU seeks to integrate free individuals into the AFSJ. Solidarity emerges not through the collective distribution of wealth, but arises from anxiety which has become a powerful political force within the AFSJ. Consequently, for those who want to resist the construction of freedom in the AFSJ around the objectification of immigration as something abject, the central normative question thus becomes one of how to challenge, re-order or desecuritize a society premised upon the advanced liberal logic of security.

6
Unmaking Security, Remaking Belonging

> [T]he refugee raises the question of association beyond, outside, in the margins, or in excess of, established political sociation, because the refugee is by definition asocial, apolitical. Being political, or as one might say the being of politics, is profoundly at issue here, in and through the presence of the refugee.
>
> Michael Dillon

Introduction: From unmasking to unmaking security

Previous chapters have unmasked security as a deficient and ineffective policy paradigm with pernicious political effects. They largely supported the view that security has a poor problem-solving record which, ironically, may well have contributed to the conditions they sought to end – for example, increased border control has unwillingly contributed to the emergence of illegal practices such as human trafficking by organized criminal networks. It was also pointed out that continuous articulations of insecurity may eventually undermine the legitimacy of the EU as a credible political actor, as articulations of insecurity risk being interpreted as the incapacity of the EU to manage these issues effectively.

The notion that security practices are ineffective and trigger more insecurity has immediate relevance for policy-makers concerned with the development and maintenance of the EU as an AFSJ. Unfortunately, however, these chapters also pointed out that unmasking security as an ineffective mode of governing with negative ramifications for the way in which the Union organizes relations between EU-citizens and third country nationals, were not followed by attempts to unmake security as the dominant framework. In fact, since the 1970s security has become an increasingly important technology for constituting freedom and upholding the Union's liberal way of life. One of the reasons, arguably, is that the identification of failure and inefficiencies will often not encourage a move away from security but, rather, lead to the development of security measures that do not suffer from identified deficiencies. The introduction of a picture and biometric data on visa are good examples of how the failure of passports in stemming immigration flows has led to the deployment of new technologies for the identification and authorization of their bearers. Similarly, pre-frontier control by means of carrier sanctions, liaison officers and the camp are all technologies that seek to repair the inefficiencies of traditional border control.

A second, closely related reason is that calls for unmaking security lose their appeal as soon as security measures can actually be shown to be effective. While it is doubtful that security measures will ever be constitutive of freedom in the AFSJ (as Chapter 5 showed, freedom is not a pre-social category but a relationship between those who govern and those who are governed), security practices can always claim to be effective in relation to the limited technical goals that they are set to achieve. For instance, readmission agreements, pre-frontier control, carrier sanctions, liaison officers, transit processing and knowledge-based border management may all be considered effective when they succeed in keeping immigrants from arriving on EU territory. Indeed, the mere conversion towards a 'best practice' regime, regardless of the actual outcomes of that regime, may be considered a success in a system where the management of immigration increasingly revolves around the coordination and communication between abstract systems of risk management.

The overarching problem is that unmasking security as ineffective will always be framed in terms of more or less security. This downplays, however, the more profound question of whether or not social issues should be securitized at all. The feedback effects security has upon society are not discussed. To unmask is not to unmake. Instrumental arguments about ineffectiveness may well prove ineffective themselves in dismantling a politics of security.

How, then, to unmake security and resist its pernicious effects on distributing belonging in EU-Europe? This final chapter seeks to work out the implications of a politics of belonging that does not function by turning the other into a risk. Following Aradau's (2004) claim that unmaking security should have a universal address and recognition, this chapter calls for the development of a European belonging that is not organized around fear of the other but around the universal values of freedom, equality and justice.

This chapter begins by exploring the Copenhagen School's notion of desecuritization as well as its recent uptake in appeals for multiculturalism and minority rights. Although the multicultural emphasis on difference and tolerance would seem to benefit third country nationals, this chapter concludes that multiculturalism fails to unmake security in a satisfactory way. Unfortunately, it remains firmly wedded to a vision of the political rooted in the friend/enemy division and agonistic difference. Arguing that unmaking security is a demonstration of sameness and equality rather than a recognition of differences, this chapter moves to the *sans-papiers* struggle for the regularization of all undocumented immigrants in Europe as a local practice of unmaking security. The *sans-papiers* struggled not for the transferral of rights upon immigrants or for the right treatment of outsiders but rather for the development of a European belonging that is not organized around a fear of the other but around the universal values of freedom, equality and justice.

Unmaking security as managing multiculturalism

Aware of the political effects of security upon society, the Copenhagen School has argued that securitization, at least in principle, should be resisted. Instead, they opt for the desecuritization of social relations. Although the Copenhagen School has been criticized for not unpacking the notion of desecuritization to the same extent as that of securitization, it would be more appropriate to say that their refusal to say much about the normative contents of desecuritization directly follows from their recognition that the choice between securitization and desecuritization is a political choice that can only be made within the particular context where such a choice is required:[1]

> To act politically means to take responsibility for leaving an impact, for forcing things in one direction instead of another. Whether such an act is 'good' or 'bad' is not defined by any inner qualities of the act or its premises, but by its effects ... [P]olitics and

> responsibility can involve prevention and limitation and, at times, the tool of *securitisation* may seem necessary (Wæver 1995: 76, emphasis in original).

The problem of how to channel violence, argues Wæver, will sometimes 'point to scenarios sufficiently worrisome that responsibility will entail securitization in order to block the worst' (Wæver 2000: 285). While the Copenhagen School generally opts for desecuritization, Wæver thus admits that in some cases securitization may politically be the more responsible thing to do.[2]

Recent arguments linking the concept of desecuritization to the themes of multiculturalism and minority rights draw upon a similar understanding of desecuritization (Roe 2004; Sasse 2005; Jutila 2006). While these authors disagree with each other in certain respects, they concur that a minority can only guarantee its identity by securitizing it to a certain degree. Demarcating the minority identity from what is viewed as threatening is a necessary evil for all minorities. Unmaking security, upon this view, would result in the death of the minority as an independent identity. Concerned with the fate of minorities, securitization is the most responsible thing to do, even if it is not without drawbacks:

> Recognizing minority rights has obvious dangers. The language of minority rights has been used and abused not only by Nazis, but also by apologists for racial segregation and apartheid. It has also been used by intolerant and belligerent nationalists and fundamentalists throughout the world to justify the domination of people outside their group, and the suppression of dissenters within the group (Kymlicka 2006: 6).

In contrast to Sasse (2005), who seems blind to the 'obvious dangers' of multiculturalism, Roe and Jutila insist on the careful management of different identities in fragile, multicultural societies. The crucial task, they argue, is to make sure that securitization processes are held within bounds and do not overcook.

Nevertheless, the problem with multiculturalism is more structural than they suggest. Although it is true that the language of minority rights may be abused for non-democratic purposes, multiculturalism, as an idea and form of organization, views the world as made up of different groups that do and should not interfere with each other.

Rather than mutual recognition and dialogue, multiculturalism, by its very nature, contributes to the image that identities are incompatible, non-univocal and antagonistic (Balibar 2002: 155). The idea of various identities co-existing under one political framework precludes that minorities – who have to accept the overall political, economic and societal framework of the society that determines their existence as a separate identity (Roe 2004: 293) – can make political demands that do not just relate to their minority status but to the foundational and substantial values upon which overall society is based. It disavows the possibility of a cross-cultural, democratic struggle for a different way of organizing society.

If the language of minority rights seems to celebrate difference by drawing attention to the claims of minorities, it also risks reinforcing the difference between minority and majority. In an already heavily securitized context, inscriptions of difference are not unlikely to support and add to processes of security that are based upon and exploit similar categorizations of 'us' and 'them'.[3] A position – whether this is conceptualized as a tragic choice inherent to politics (Wæver 2000) or in terms of a defence of minority rights (Jutila 2006, Roe 2004) – that mobilizes new and more pressing insecurities is undesirable. It entails that a particular grouping of a security figuration can be questioned but never the antagonistic logic of the security figuration itself. For if securitization presupposes exclusion, then every positive articulation of security ('protection of minority rights') will automatically lead to the institutionalization of a new, yet equally absolute, antagonistic difference.

Moreover, in the case of *undocumented* immigration, the position of multiculturalism is undesirable for an additional reason. Multiculturalism operates from the premise that groups are already constituted and recognized as separate identities, but has no answer to the claims of the non-recognized multitude. Undocumented immigrants, constituted as illegal or abject beings, are not officially recognized by the society in which they live and work. Thus, while some have proposed the Habermasian idea of communicative action as a way of unmaking securitized relationships between self and other (Williams 2003), illegalized immigrants are not considered legitimate discussion partners. In the words of Rancière:

> The immigrant is first and foremost a worker who has lost his name, a worker who is no longer perceived as such. Instead of the worker

> or proletarian who is the object of an acknowledged wrong and a subject who vents his grievance in a struggle and disputation, the immigrant appears as at once the perpetrator of an expiable wrong and the cause of a problem calling for the round-table treatment (Rancière 1995: 105).

Without a chair, Rancière argues, the shape of the table matters little. This is not to insist, of course, that argumentative procedures and the inclusion of pro-immigration NGOs in decision-making have not improved the lot of (undocumented) immigrants. To the contrary, new civic values have appeared within the EU as a result of the lobbying of immigrant movements such as the European Council for Refugees and Exiles and the European Migrants Forum (Withol de Wenden 1999). The problem is rather that immigrants are denied the possibility to express themselves, while those that speak on their behalf often can only do so because they have been recognized as their legitimate interlocutors by political attribution (Sciortino 2000: 224).

Huysmans (1998: 588), therefore, has suggested a political aesthetics of everydayness which seeks to contextualize security questions within wider economic and social practices that frame immigrants as individuals engaged in complex daily meditations. According to him, such counter frames defy the simple us – them reasoning inherent in security talk. The point of these alternative stories is to make us aware that everyday experiences and human interactions are informed and moulded by broader political and social settings that cannot be solved by securitization. This strategy goes beyond the cultural categorizing implied by the multicultural framework and emphasizes that immigrants are not so much 'immigrants' as 'workers', 'wives', 'parents', 'athletes' or 'students'. Although it certainly would be useful to tell these different stories, it is uncertain how successful these would be in the EU context where security, too, has taken on an everyday form insofar as the AFSJ increasingly takes a point of departure in the anxieties, fears and misgivings of EU citizens, Indeed, the AFSJ may well have given birth to what Isin elsewhere has described as 'the neurotic citizen':

> We have seen that what the neurotic subject wants is the impossible. It wants absolute security. It wants absolute safety ... Yet, since it has also been promised the impossible, it cannot address

> its illusions ... The need to eliminate necessity or anxiety from its existence turns its wants into claims. In essence, these claims are impossible because they articulate rights that cannot exist ... The neurotic citizen has been promised so much and developed such unrealistic sense of its rights that it becomes confused about its actual and actualisable rights. The formation of neurotic claims reproduces illusions of the neurotic citizen and enables it to shift responsibility to objects outside itself with hostility (Isin 2004: 233, 234).

Although a political aesthetics of everyday life may have important desecuritizing effects in cases where security is defined as an exceptional discourse removed from, rather than embedded in, everyday social, economic and political practices, its potential to unmake security is perhaps less significant when insecurity, anxiety and neurotic vigilance already overdetermine daily interactions.

Nonetheless, Huysmans' strategy points at an important issue. It stresses the agency of immigrants and the functions they fulfil in societies as general members. While Huysmans' strategy emphasizes difference, he does not succumb to the multicultural seduction to divide belonging along the particular lines of cultural, religious or ethnic membership. As such, he invokes a logic that is universal rather than exclusionary, political rather than neurotic. Aradau has further stressed these elements in her account of unmaking security as emancipation.

Unmaking security as enforcing universality

Aradau's (2004; 2007) focus on desecuritization as emancipation should not be taken to imply the final move towards a harmonious society free of domination, power and fault-lines. Obviously, that would only replicate the neurotic illusion of absolute security in a perfectly harmonious society. The point of an emancipatory process is not to provide a blueprint for the good life; rather, emancipation is always a local, situational struggle to re-create the relations that have been fixed along the exclusionary lines of security (Aradau 2004: 402). By this Aradau means that unmaking security ultimately is a struggle for the universal principles that are already present within society and by means of which a society identifies itself. While these values are defined as universal, the struggle exists in demonstrating that security practices exclude certain groups from enjoying these universal rights and benefits (Aradau 2004: 403).

To work this out in slightly more concrete terms, Aradau suggests that such a strategy plays itself out on two levels. First, she shows that those that are marginalized can demonstrate the gap between official discourse and actual practices. However, she adds, this strategy is only open to those that are already present as part of the community upon which they make their claims bear. An important precondition for emancipation, therefore, is a pre-existing common belonging to a political community. When others are not acknowledged as part of society (e.g., undocumented immigrants), unmaking security takes on a different form. In such cases, desecuritization becomes a strategy of dis-identification. That is, those that do not belong first have to dis-identify with the identity bestowed upon them ('illegal immigrants') in order then to partake in a recognized universal struggle (for workers, women, prostitutes, etc.).

To a large degree, I agree with Aradau that dis-identification can provide useful ways of unmaking security. However, I would like to add that dis-identification is not the only way to perform a desecuritizing act. Instead of dis-identification, one could also imagine a situation where the excluded explicitly identify with their excluded position in a struggle for the 'right to have rights'. The aim of such a struggle is to show that the true measurement of universal belonging lies not in an abstract 'universal' ideal, but in the ways in which a community relates to its abject. In contrast to securitizing processes with the aim of establishing a sense of *immunity* vis-à-vis the abject, such act of unmaking security take point of departure in the abject as the point from which to articulate new forms of *community*. The *sans-papier* (literally 'without papers') struggle, where outsiders have claimed rights without any prior recognition, illustrates that such identification can promote the development of new bonds of belonging between self and other.

The struggle of the *sans-papiers* movement opens up for a re-imagination of political structures in Europe along the emancipatory lines sketched above. The current *sans-papiers* movement started on 18 March 1996 when 300 African men, women and children occupied churches to stop deportations of undocumented immigrants from French territory. While the *sans-papiers* movement originally began as a particular French phenomenon in response to the laws enacted there, the movement has taken on a wider European dimension when the movement started to demand the regularization of *sans-papiers* in Europe, claiming 'papers for all *sans-papiers* in Europe' (Callaway and Martin 1998).

From the beginning, the movement was well aware of the fact that such an emancipatory struggle could not be waged by others, but required that they themselves emerged from their minority status and put an obligation on the political community for their recognition. As Madgiguène Cissé, one of the leading delegates of the *sans-papiers*, argues: 'We demand our regularisation. We are not in hiding. We have come out into the daylight' (Cissé 1997). It was thus not through a process of dis-identification but exactly by identifying with their position as undocumented migrants that the *sans-papiers* left behind their illegality and claimed their place in the social order. The desecuritizing force of the *sans-papiers* movement is located in their demands to be granted those rights precisely *as* undocumented immigrants. Thus Madjiguène Cissé argues that 'the struggle taught us first of all to be autonomous':

> There were organizations which came to support us and which were used to helping immigrants in struggle. They were also used to acting as the relay between immigrants in struggle and the authorities, and therefore more or less to manage the struggle. They would tell us, 'Right, we the organizations have made an appointment to explain this or that'; and we had to say, 'But we can explain it very well ourselves.' ... If we had not taken our autonomy, we would not be here today, because there really have been many organizations telling us we could never win, that we could not win over public opinion because people were not ready to hear what we had to say (Cissé 1997).

Cissé (2003) explains that when the *sans-papiers* first occupied the Saint-Ambroise church, representatives of immigrant right organizations came to tell them to return to their hiding places and to let these organizations speak on their behalf. The *sans-papiers*, however, refused with the argument that they had to make themselves count if they wanted to be accounted for as part of the community.

Contra to immigrant right organizations, which tried to negotiate with the government for a regularization of the *sans-papiers* on a case by case basis, the *sans-papiers* explicitly refused partial regularizations in an attempt to counteract the division of immigrants in 'good' and 'bad' movement or '*bogus*' and '*bona fide*' asylum-seekers fixed along security lines. Instead, the *sans-papiers* claimed the 'right to papers for all' – replicating in other terms the Arendtian struggle for the right to have rights, i.e. the right to be recognized as a political subject belonging to the community (Arendt 1958).

The protests and civil obedience of the *sans-papiers* constitute an important dilemma for liberal democracies which adhere to the rule of law. From the viewpoint of the rule of law, the struggle of the *sans-papiers* is illegitimate insofar as protests and demonstrations are seen as a disturbance of the public order with irrupting effects on the fabric of society. The rule of law, which is intended to protect the people not only against arbitrary decisions by the executive branches of government but also from the passions of the mob, plays an important role in the promotion of peaceful relations within society. Hence, as was shown in the introduction, hunger strikes and other forms of protest and civil disobedience are often interpreted as a form of blackmail by those who, by effect of their non-membership, have no legal right to do so. Too many exceptions to the rule of law – be it in the form of a Schmittian exception of the sovereign or by a revolutionary bottom-up process – thus risk rendering the rule of law meaningless as an important guarantee for freedom and a block against social instability and civil violence.

However, the complexity of the struggle of the *sans-papiers* cannot be captured under the simple banner of irrational and unrestrained mass politics. Although it is true that 'too much unrestrained power for the people may reduce the space for contesting different opinions about substantive values that is guaranteed by the law and which implies a minimum level of freedom and equality' (Huysmans 2004b: 335), the emancipatory struggle of the *sans-papiers* is precisely *not* a struggle for new substantial values for the community. Rather – and this is where the strategy of identification merges with Aradau's view on desecuritization as exposing a gap between discourse and practice – the *sans-papiers* struggle proceeds by the identification of gaps and inconsistencies between these official legal principles such as freedom, freedom of movement and justice and the actual practices which contradict these official values. Thus, their struggle represents a moment where the *sans-papiers* declare themselves as equal, 'though aware that they have no fundamental right to do so save the appeal to what has been inscribed earlier, which their actions raises behind it as a banner' (Rancière 1995: 162).

Thus, deliberately exploiting the ambivalence at the heart of the word 'demonstration', immigrant demonstrations are not to be understood as protests against the substantial values of the community, but as a practice that seeks to demonstrate and verify the official principles of that community. As Balibar concludes: 'To confront the hegemonic structure by denouncing the gap or contradiction between its official values and actual practice – with greater or lesser success – is the most effective way of enforcing its universality' (Balibar 2002: 162).

Accordingly, the *sans-papiers* movement did not ask for new rights but rather pointed out that the universal values of 'justice', 'freedom', 'human rights' and 'freedom of movement' that underpin the official discourses of the AFSJ have been denied to them in actual practice. Or as Madjiguène Cissé states in an interview: 'Human rights apply to every person. When these rights are under threat, it is legitimate to struggle to have them *reinstated* ... Freedom of movement is not something invented. It *confirms* an existing situation ... One day, "those without papers" in Saint-Amboise requested precisely the *acknowledgment* of that situation' (Cissé 1999: emphasis added).

While securitizing practices constituted undocumented immigrants as the abject falling outside the boundaries of belonging, the *sans-papiers'* claim for the right to papers for all sought to impose an obligation on the other to recognize their presence in the political sphere. Acknowledging their existence as the securitized other, they did thus not demand for the protection of their life in the name of human rights or any other abstract universal. Knowing that in practice the idea of human rights as a universal backdrop makes little sense when it does not enable one to exercise these rights in any meaningful way, the core objective of the *sans-papiers* movement was first and foremost to be recognized as equals (Cissé 2003), which refers to the continuous political process by which those who have been excluded 'impose a rational obligation on the other to recognize them' (Rancière 1995: 50). Confronted with a strict policing of the boundaries of European belonging, the *sans-papiers* fought thus not only for their inclusion, but also for their illegality to be embraced as '*the point of inherent exception/exclusion, the "abject", of the concrete positive order, as the only point of true universality*' (Žižek 1999: 224, emphasis in original).

While emancipation cannot happen through an external decision, this does not mean that EU-citizens cannot partake in the emancipatory struggle of the *sans-papiers*. While they cannot liberate the other, they *can* identify with their struggle through responding to the obligation to recognize the other as equal. Identification with the cause of the struggle can take many forms such as the noted resistance of airline passengers against forced removals by air or local protests against the building of immigrant detention centres. Resistance therefore needs not only support free movement of non-EU nationals, but may also point out the ways in which the freedom of EU-citizens themselves is limited by such security measures such as the recent decision to include biometric data in the passports of EU-citizens or a directive that criminalizes the facilitation of unauthorized entry, transit, residence and employment of non EU-nationals (EU Council 2002c). Such measures do not necessarily have to be seen as targeting immigrants alone, because they also infringe on EU-citizens' right to invite persons of their choice into their houses, or to employ persons of their choice within their companies.

Unmaking security as bottom-up citizenship

The *sans-papiers* struggle is thus not just about the responsible treatment of immigrants. Nor are its implications limited to the moment of demonstration. It impacts upon the very foundations upon which European belonging is founded. As we saw in earlier chapters, security practices that claim to protect values such as freedom and free movement in the AFSJ actually displace this freedom with fear of the enemy as the central principle around which belonging is organized. The *sans-papiers* movement contributes to the institutionalization of a space where these values are distributed more equally, while retaining the fundamental freedoms already inscribed in the rule of law.

As such, the struggle of the *sans-papiers* provides an important counterweight to the current organization of belonging within the EU, which is basically a top-down process where European citizenship is assigned from above on the basis of national citizenship of an EU member state. The institution of a European citizenship from above has further highlighted the difference between EU nationals and non-EU nationals, as the latter – even if they reside legally in the EU – are excluded from European citizenship. Thus while European citizenship has empowered EU-nationals against wrongful exclusions, Martiniello has been right to argue that only a successful 'pressure "from below" for a new European citizenship, could bring about an extended breach in the nationalist logic and open the way towards post-nationalism in Europe' (Martiniello 1995: 49).

The *sans-papiers* invite reflections on the development of a bottom-up citizenship. They illustrate that citizenship is more than just a status of rights bestowed on those who already are full members of the community; it is also a practice of active engagement that develops in dialogue between insiders and outsiders (Isin 2000). For a democratic Europe to emerge, integration cannot just be the process by which rights are conferred upon its members. European integration and solidarity also happens when dominated groups struggle against inequality in the very name of the values cherished by the community. The *sans-papiers* have sought to do exactly this: to create a space for the unrepresentable within presentation through the admission of abjection into the field of normality (Balibar 2004: 48). Their struggle is not one for difference but for the recognition of their 'voice' as part of the community. Their struggle, then, is one of repoliticizing European belonging from the outside, from the point of the most excluded:

> Insofar as it expresses the movement of collective emancipation, the criterion of political citizenship is the ability of a 'polity' to free itself from the forms of distribution and redistribution ('accounting'). It does not take as its objective the 'balance of profit and losses' among those who already possess something … but the constitution of a 'people' (or *dēmos*) that begins as nonexistent on account of the exclusion of those who are considered unworthy of the status of citizen (depending on the epoch and the circumstances: slaves or servants, workers or paupers, women, foreigners, and so on) (Balibar 2004: 72).[4]

Balibar refers to such a citizenship as a citizenship *without* community, meaning a form of citizenship that develops in conjunction with what is outside the community but not without relation to it (with + out). As such, the *sans-papiers* impinges upon the very exclusionary foundations upon which the scheme of European belonging is constituted. Their claim is not a claim for an extension of belonging by widening the circle of citizenship and the rights and duties that follow from it; rather, it asks for a post-national form of citizenship that is not based on the principle of nationality but on residence and the freedom of movement for *all* people: 'We struggle for freedom of movement in its most concrete meaning, such as the ability to travel and to settle, wherever we wish to, without hindrance; because this struggle concerns also the refusal of social control which afflicts us all; whether or not we have papers' (cited in Hayter 2004: 146).

In contrast to the idea of a 'European citizenship' as an abstract prerequisite for political rights, desecuritization thus refers to the process whereby belonging is mediated in a continuous political process that recognizes those who have been subjected to securitizing processes as part of the public sphere of existence. What starts out as a particular struggle for a particular group can thus be 'blown up' to a question of the future of Europe itself. The identification of the people with undocumented immigrants can articulate a space in which belonging is not passively imposed from above upon an already present population; rather, belonging is negotiated in the concrete struggle for desecuritization through which individuals actively contribute to the constitution of a European public space. 'Self-emancipation', Rancière (1995: 50) argues, 'is not secession, but self-affirmation as a joint sharer in a common world'. The struggle of the *sans-papiers*, then, is the struggle against the denial of citizenship which, somewhat paradoxically perhaps, is also an important stage (although not necessarily always successful) in the bottom-up development of an active European citizenship where new concrete bonds of solidarity are created by opening up a space of equality by means of a shared struggle for emancipation.

Conclusion

This chapter has sought to outline the contours of a strategy of desecuritization within the context of the constitution of the EU as an

AFSJ. Following Aradau, it was argued that desecuritization could be beneficially conceptualized as an emancipatory struggle on the part of undocumented immigrants for the political 'right to have rights', i.e. to become recognized as a full member of the community. The struggle of emancipation was defined not as the granting of rights to minority groups, but as the exposure of a gap between the discourses of a community and its concrete practices. This was illustrated by the struggle of the *sans-papiers* which, while transgressing the rule of law, called for their inclusion and recognition exactly on the basis of the substantive values of the community.

Strategically positioning itself as the group caught in the hole between speech and practices, the *sans-papiers* represented themselves as 'the fraction which is capable of presenting its own emancipation (or as that fraction which, in continuing in … alienation, inevitably entails the unfreedom of all)' (Balibar 2002: 6). As the *sans-papiers* movement illustrated, emancipation is not the adherence to some sort of universal ideal on which the community should be founded (not even if this ideal is, as with Habermas, only procedural) but on the verification, demonstration and re-inscription of the values to which a community already adheres. Understood in these terms, the unmaking of security has no natural or historical endpoint but is always materialized in the concrete struggle between insiders and outsiders. Thus while desecuritization calls for an emancipatory struggle and a restructuring of social relations, it also acknowledges that '[t]here will always be antagonisms, struggles' and that the 'myth of the transparent and homogeneous society – which implies the end of politics – must be resolutely abandoned' (Laclau and Mouffe 1990: 130).

The point of emancipation is thus not to overcome these struggles and to work towards a consensus but to recognize that a coming together can only happen in conflict. Most importantly, though, the interpretation of desecuritization as a struggle for emancipation shows the ways in which equality, freedom and justice can replace a fear of the other as the energetic principle around which a community is organized. While anxiety is an increasingly powerful political force in the constitution of the AFSJ, it reifies and increases the gap between the official values of the AFSJ and the concrete practices by means of which it is maintained and developed. Ultimately, therefore, the struggle for desecuritization is about how to retain freedom, justice and equality as the organizing principle for politics within the EU. Adding European citizenship to the national forms which already exist is a first step towards creating solidarity on a European level, but is incomplete as long as it is not followed by a bottom-up struggle for citizenship which effects a bond between all inhabitants as concrete progress in the history of the rights of man.

7
Conclusion: The EU as an Area of Security, Security and . . . Security

The security policies underpinning the AFSJ rest on shaky assumptions. They lack democratic accountability, judicial legitimacy and are largely ineffective in bringing about a Union closer to its citizens. Complex divisions of competences continue to exist between the different pillars, contributing to legal uncertainty and unaccountability.

This is unlikely to change in the near or mid-term future. While some have argued that the inclusion of the Fundamental Charter of Human Rights in the Constitutional Treaty could rectify some of these problems (Carrera and Guild 2006), the French and Dutch 'no' has squashed such hopes in an early stadium. Yet, even if a Fundamental Charter of Human Rights would be added to the EU-treaty, it is uncertain if asylum-seekers, undocumented immigrants and would-be immigrants would gain much from it. While the Charter would have provided a much needed democratic check on the legal measures adopted, universal rights are not a sufficient condition for emancipation and more universal belonging. Universality, as illustrated by the struggle of the *sans-papiers*, always needs to be enforced by those excluded from it.

Similarly, while few would dispute that a clearer division of competences in the Area of Freedom, Security and Justice as envisaged in the Constitutional Treaty would have been a welcome development, the discussion of the Maastricht and especially Amsterdam Treaty showed that a transferral of competences from security actors to other experts such as the European Commission does not automatically unmake the security frame. In fact, while Maastricht and Amsterdam could have had some dislocating effects upon the interpretation of immigration, both instead strengthened the symbolic authority of security professionals to speak and define immigration.

Today, the risk management of immigration exists of expensive and expanding webs of control. While their effectiveness is questionable, the Hague Programme, a multiannual programme set in motion in November 2004 to follow up on the Tampere framework (1999–2004), gives high priority to these security measures. Although the Hague Programme talks about strengthening freedom (paragraphs 7–17), strengthening security (paragraphs 18–26) and strengthening justice (paragraphs 27–32), a closer reading of the document reveals that freedom and justice are overdetermined by the meaning of security. Freedom is discussed mainly in negative terms, as threats to freedom that should be neutralized. Similarly, justice refers not to the procedural or substantive equality of people residing in the EU, but to a means in the hand of the administration that enables it to act swiftly against these threats. In an ironic remark, Bigo observed that it perhaps would be better to 'adapt the titles to their actual content by renaming the three parts: 1. strengthening security, 2. strengthening security, 3. strengthening security' (Bigo 2006: 35).

For Balzacq and Carrera (2006), this development stands in sharp contrast with the 1999 Tampere European Council, which, they claimed, stroke a better balance between security and freedom. This book has suggested otherwise. The 'Area of Security, Security and Security' did not just blossom up in The Hague; its seeds were sown in the 1970s, its flowers sprouted in Maastricht and Amsterdam. Alternative discourses, such as those on free movement, foreign policy and development, have never been able to fully penetrate the institutions of decision-making. For example, the foreign affairs objective of addressing the root causes of immigration was quickly subordinated to the management of immigration and asylum flows in third countries, where development priorities have been attuned to security concerns.

Indeed, the apparent contradiction between the liberal focus on freedom on the one hand and the strong reliance on security on the other can be explained by the specific liberal mode of governing, where risk management takes centre stage as the technology through which to guarantee autonomy, freedom and mobility. While they are often seen as competing (Lavenex 2001), economic, humanitarian and foreign affairs discourses often complement and confirm the risk approach. They generally accept that immigration is a risk, but argue that *some* sub-categories should be excluded from such a focus. For instance, humanitarians may argue that security measures are at the expense of 'good' asylum-seekers, while economic discourses have pointed out that not all immigrants are undesirable 'free-riders' and 'opportunists'. Nevertheless, in arguing so, both confirm the security norm against which these outliers are to be measured. Claiming that exceptions need to be made, they (unwillingly) contribute to targeted risk management that depends on these very categorizations.[1]

As a specific liberal tendency of governing through risk, the securitization of immigration in the EU could be said to be part of a broader trend in advanced liberal societies. Much indicates, at least, that governing mobility through risk is a global concern (Bauman 1998; Bauman 2004). The highly technological profiling at the US-Mexican border, the American USVISIT program as well as the building of immigrant camps in Australia show that similar techniques are deployed in liberal states outside the EU. According to Bauman (1998), this is the result of the emergence of a global consumer society to which people have differentiated access. Although wealth certainly is an important element in establishing who constitutes an 'immigration risk' (see Chapter 5), the securitization of immigration in the EU has followed a specific trajectory where immigrants have been linked to the internal market, free movement and freedom in the AFSJ – referent objects specific to the EU and with little resonance outside the European context. The obsession with security cannot just be explained in macro-terms by pointing at the existence of a global consumer society. Obviously, the Europeanization of immigration as a security problem is part and parcel of a wider global development. Yet, the institutional processes, discourses and practices by which immigrants have been constituted as dangerous are local rather than global. Empirical knowledge about the local conditions under which certain issues have been rendered governable within a security calculus may help us understand the compare and contrast governance in the EU with the technologies of power and resistance in other liberal regimes.

The increasing routinization of security as a core technique in promoting freedom in the AFSJ brings up some conceptual questions regarding the realist rationality of security as an exceptional discourse. At first sight, the exceptional act seems to have become increasingly unimportant in the EU, as security has been de-dramatized under liberal rationalities of governance. Contrary to the geopolitical image of security and war, techniques of risk management cut across place and time and govern mobility through markers of legitimacy and illegitimacy. While processes of securitization have not disappeared, they generally remain short of the securitizing act or decision that defines the threshold between the social order and the state of exception. Michael Williams (2003: 521) thus speaks of a continuum running from risk to existential threat, where the state of exception or the act of securitization is viewed only as the most extreme response to problems which are generally governed by less extreme forms of security policy.

However, this book has pointed at a slightly more complex relationship between risk and security, exception and normality. Under advanced liberal conditions, the exception seems not to have disappeared; rather the exception has become the rule. The notion that the state of exception now coincides with the normal order has been most systematically pursued by the Italian philosopher Giorgio Agamben (1998; 2005; see also Dean (2007); Ericson (2007)). According to him, modern Western societies are characterized by a permanent state of exception in which law and fact enter into a zone of indistinction. In this zone of indistinction, the central figure one encounters is that of *homo sacer*, bare life stripped of all its value in the sense that violence against him/her remains unpunished. This zone, he argues, is symbolized by the camp, which exemplifies the space that is opened up when the state of exception finds a more permanent location:

> The camp is thus the structure in which the state of exception – the possibility of deciding on which founds sovereign power – is realized *normally* ... [It] actually delimits a space in which the normal order is de facto suspended and in which whether or not atrocities are committed depends not on the law but on the civility and ethical sense of the police who temporarily act as sovereign (Agamben 1998: 170, 174, emphasis in original).

This argument is highly relevant for understanding the governance of immigration by risk. Airport detention centres, exit centres and off-shore protection and transit processing centres can and have all been described as the institutionalization of a permanent exception to national and international legal arrangements (Noll 2003; Rajaram and Grundy-Warr 2004; Diken and Laustsen 2005).

Furthermore, while immigrants are of course not *homini sacri* in the sense that they can be killed without punishment,[2] they are nevertheless included in the law only as something to be excluded, i.e. as abject individuals without the right to have rights. This exclusion of the immigrant from the juridical order coincides with Bigo's (2002; see also Chapter 5) characterization of current security practices as constituting a *ban*opticon, where certain groups, which are not considered as legal subjects, are subjected to exclusionary and pro-active forms of power. For Agamben, too, the structure of the 'ban' is exemplary to the state of exception which 'holds life in its ban by abandoning it' (Agamben 1998: 29). The production of the abject, in turn, is a direct consequence of the Union's framing of the security and freedom nexus. Within the EU, the state of exception increasingly appears as the dominant paradigm of governing. Contra to the realist rendering of security, the securitization of immigration illustrates that 'the state of exception has gradually been replaced by an unprecedented generalization of the paradigm of security as the normal technique of government' (Agamben 2005: 14). This reading of the state of exception as a paradigm of governing, in turn, seems to match the 'information-governance paradox' described in Chapter 5. This paradox pointed to the fact that limited and targeted forms of risk intervention may become self-perpetuating and self-reinforcing, because they fuel a continuous demand for more information and intelligence which in turn leads to more detailed forms of risk regulation, risk communication and risk management. The state of exception has become designed into the flow of everyday life as part of risk governance.

Pre-frontier control (visa, carrier sanctions, liaison officers), buffer zones (transit processing centres, offshore protection zones) and knowledge-based border management (biometrics, information governance) have become key sites of risk profiling with the overall aim of segregating 'trusted travellers' from 'risky migrants'. Assumptions of normality and abnormality govern mobilities by producing norms of behaviour with deviance (e.g., paying airline tickets by cash, running through the airport) being codified as risk indicators. If Agamben is right that the state of exception has returned as a technique of governing, risky places such as the airport may well be considered as a 'micro-cosmos' for how people are governed in the wider societal setting (Salter 2008).

Yet, security knowledge, however mundane, inherently re-iterates particular views of the legitimate scope and form of politics. It is a struggle over competing opinions of the good life and the allocation of values, rights and duties. To recapture this link between security and the political, therefore, European Studies should resist the temptation to accept the displacement of immigration as a risk to the internal market and free movement at face value. As the framing of immigrants as a threat is connected to views of the good life, it was shown that the question 'to securitize or not to securitize?' cannot (and should not) be subsumed under an instrumental interpretation alone but also has to include a normative discussion of how to organize belonging in the political community. In this respect, the struggle of the *sans papiers* should help us theorize, recognize and support the bottom-up instances of European citizenship through which we recognize the contours of a more democratic EU-polity with freedom and equality, rather than fear and insecurity, as its organizing principles.

Notes

Chapter 1

1. For instance, Germany signed recruitment agreements with Italy, Spain and Greece (1960), Turkey (1961), Portugal (1964), Tunisia (1965) and Morocco (1966). The Netherlands concluded similar agreements with Italy (1960), Spain (1961), Portugal (1963), Turkey (1964), Greece (1966), Morocco (1969), Yugoslavia (1970) and Tunisia (1970) (Geddes 2003).
2. In fact, third country nationals working in the EU also benefited from the social entitlement provisions laid down in this Regulation, which gave them access to national education systems. Furthermore, the European Court of Justice ruled that not only foreign workers but also their spouses were entitled to these rights regardless of their nationality (Geddes 2000: 157). For more detail, see the *Dzodi v. Belgium* case (C-297/88 and C-197/89 [1990] ECR 3783) and the *Kziber* case (C-18/90 [1991] ECR I-199).
3. Lahav (2004b; 2004a) has argued that the narrow focus on economic elite opinion should be replaced with a broader focus on mass public opinion, which is generally less favourable towards third country immigration than elite opinion. Yet, European mass public opinion is itself structured, framed and mediated by various discourses and policies. What Lahav ignores in her account is that opinion polls not just passively measure some pre-existing opinions. They are also instruments that react to, express, condition and influence a political agenda.
4. See Boswell (2003a: 100), Mitsilegas et al. (2003), Müller (2003), Occhipinti (2003: 5, 11), Wagner (2003: 1036), de Lobkowicz (2002), Fortescue (2002: 8), Lodge (2002), Knelangen (2001), Monar (2001: 754), Stetter (2000: 81), Hix (1999: 314), Guyomarch (1997: 137) and Callovi (1992).
5. See Crawford (2002: 35), Guyomarch (1997: 140), Anderson (1995: 131), Hebenton (1995: 141) and Benyon et al. (1994: 48).
6. See, e.g., De Genova (2002), Andreas (2000: 9) and Bigo (1994).
7. See, e.g., Guiraudon (2000; 2001), Lahav (1998) and Bigo (1996). See also Chapter 2.
8. As Huysmans summarizes, the doctrine of political realism 'retrieves the ordering force of the fear of violent death by a mythical replay of variations of the Hobbesian state of nature' (Huysmans 1998: 571).
9. As the 1999 Amsterdam Treaty stipulates that the institutional arrangements for cooperation in the field of immigration apply for a five-year period (1999–2004), this project will not focus upon the 2000 Nice IGC because its impact upon the framing of immigration was minimal.

Chapter 2

1. Cited in Baldwin-Edwards and Hebenton (1994: 137).
2. Articles 7 (illegal immigration) and 8 (drug trafficking) mention the need for compensatory measures in the short run, while article 17 (illegal immigration) refers to the need for measures applicable in the long term. Article 9 calls for the exchange of information, while article 10 urges the signatory states to regularly hold meetings on these matters.
3. Also the bilateral Neustadt/Aisch agreement which preceded the signing of Schengen was signed by the Ministers of Transport. The Schengen Accord was signed by F.W. van Eekelen (the Netherlands), Goebbels (Luxembourg), Lalumière (France), Schreckenberger (Germany) and de Keersmaeker (Belgium) (see Schengen Agreement 1985).
4. Moreover, both Wallace (1999: 512) and Jobard (1999) suggest that political elites were quick to respond to the strike because it blocked their access to ski resorts in the Alps.
5. Entscheidend ist vielmehr, dass in der Perzeption der maßgeblichen Akteure der nationalen Innen- bzw. Justizministerien sowie hochrangiger Vertreter der polizeilichen Praxis die Grenzen ein zentrales Element der Kriminalitetsbekämpfung darstellten, deren Preisgabe deshalb allenfalls hingenommen werden könne, wenn sie durch polizeiliche 'Ausgleichmaßnahmen' flankiert werde (Knelangen 2001: 104).
6. The origins of the name Trevi are somewhat unclear. According to some, the name refers to Bernini's famous fountain where the justice and home affairs ministers had their group picture taken in 1975. Others have pointed out that the name in fact refers to the Italian minister Fontana or the Dutch minister A.R. Fonteijn. Ex post facto, the name Trevi was said to be the French acronym for Terrorisme, Radicalisme, Extrémisme et Violence Internationale (see Bigo 1996: 86-87; Knelangen 2001: 91; Lavenex 2001: 143; Occhipinti 2003: 31).
7. In 1985, 'Trevi III' was established with the aim of enhancing cooperation on serious crime, while in 1988, a fourth working group, 'Trevi 92', was launched to deal with the internal security consequences of the abolishment of internal borders in Europe (see below). For an overview of the formal structures of Trevi, see, among others, Rupprecht and Hellenthal (1992: 151–153), Benyon et al. (1993: 152–165, 237–241), Bonnefoi (1994: 21-28), Anderson et al. (1995: 53–56), Ahnfelt and From (1996: 60–67), Bigo (1996: 86–88, 155–163), Guyomarch (1997: 131–133), Knelangen (2001: 88–99), Mitsilegas (2003: 29–31) and Occhipinti (2003: 40–46).
8. These meetings took place in London (1977), Bonn (1978), Dublin (1979), London (1981), Bonn (1983) and Rome (1985).
9. For instance, in 1977 a group of Palestinians hijacked a Lufthansa airplane in the so-called Schleyer kidnapping in an attempt to force the West-German authorities to release prisoners of the RAF (see Mitsilegas, Monar et al. 2003: 21).

10. The Court in turn confirmed that the Commission had no constitutional competence to prevent the members from implementing drafts it did not consider in accordance with community policies (European Court of Justice 1987). The cases of Denmark, The Netherlands and the United Kingdom were ruled inadmissible by the European Court of Justice because they were presented after the deadline for submission had expired.
11. The official, but much longer title of what is popularly known as the Dublin Convention is: Convention Determining the State Responsible for Examining Applications for Asylum Lodged in one of the Member States of the European Communities. The Dublin Convention was not ratified until August 1997.
12. See also Weldes' (1996) for a discussion of the importance of the concept of 'national interest' as an important legitimating device.
13. See also Huysmans (2004b) on the tenuous relationship between exceptional politics and the liberal democratic separation of powers. The ethical dimension of European internal security will be dealt with in more detail in Chapter 5.
14. This did not prevent the European Parliament from criticizing the democratic unaccountability of the agreement from the sideline. The democratic deficit of the Schengen negotiation process also formed the basis for the European Parliament's 1989 advice against ratification (cf. Knelangen 2001: 110, n 125).
15. For a brief account on the ratification process of Schengen in the diverse states, see Benyon et al. (1993: 138–140).
16. Moreover, even if the European Parliament or any other actor had discussed these questions in relation to the introduction of the internal market, it is doubtful whether this would have effectively countered security discourses. At the time, the perceived security consequences were hypothetical (because they were located in the future) and it would have been difficult, therefore, for non-security actors to challenge the scenarios, knowledge, calculations and discourses of the security experts.
17. The interview was conducted and digitally transcribed in Danish. The translation is mine.

Chapter 3

1. For comprehensive overviews of the Maastricht IGC (member state positions, bargaining strategies, supranational entrepreneurship, etc.) see, among others, Doutriaux (1992), Laursen and Vanhoonacker (1992), Cloos et al. (1993), Duff et al. (1994), Moravscik (1998) and Beach (2002a).
2. For a collection of documents calling for the launch of a political union, see the annexes attached to Laursen and Vanhoonacker (1992).
3. For a more detailed overview of the member state positions, see Laursen et al. (1992) and Knelangen (2001: 145–149). Holding the Presidency, the Luxembourg government did not make its own preferences public.

However, as member of both the Schengen framework and the Benelux free zone, it is likely that also Luxembourg would have opted for an increased role of the community institutions.

4. In the end only Belgium would support the Dutch proposal (Laursen, Vanhoonacker et al. 1992: 18).
5. The basic disagreement between the two camps is reflected in the legal instruments at the disposal of the JHA pillar. To a considerable extent, these instruments underscore the disagreement as to whether the EU should legislate at all in this area. For while article K.3.2(a) and article K.3.2(b) of the treaty allow the Council to adopt 'joint positions' and 'joint actions', they are only allowed to do so if the objectives of the joint positions or actions cannot be reached by the member states alone (the principle of subsidiarity). The Council could also draw up conventions (article K.3.2(c)), but these conventions – while binding on the international level – did not necessarily have an effect upon national law (depending on a country's domestic rules on this).
6. The K.4 Committee is composed of national representatives of each member state. Generally, these representatives are the same persons that were part of the Coordinators' Group for Free Movement. As such, the K.4 Committee is made up of staff members of the national ministries of the interior, although in France an administrative unit to coordinate all K.4 Committee affairs was set up under the Office of the Prime Minister. However, also here the Ministry of the Interior retained a lot of its influence because of its right to nominate a candidate for the position of K.4 official that both presides over the agency set up under the Prime Minister and participates in the K.4 Committee (Niemeier 1995: 325–326).
7. The third Steering Group on Judicial Cooperation emerged out of the frame of the EPC (European Political Community). As this group has not dealt significantly with the topic of immigration, it falls outside the scope of this book.
8. See article K.4.1 of the Maastricht Treaty.
9. On the establishment of CIREA and CIREFI, see the Decision establishing the clearing house (CIREA), adopted by the ministers responsible for immigration on 30-11-1992 and 01-12-1992 in London, SN 2836/93 WG1 1505; and the Decision setting up a Centre for Information, Discussion and Exchange on the Crossing of Borders and Immigration (CIREFI), adopted by the ministers responsible for immigration on 30-11-1992 in London.
10. On databases as discourse, see Poster (1996) and Ericson and Haggerty (1997).
11. See article K.6 of Title VI of the Maastricht Treaty.
12. The 'Declaration on Asylum' attached to the Maastricht Treaty stipulated that 'the Council will consider as a matter of priority questions concerning Member States' asylum policies, with the aim of adopting, by the beginning of 1993, common actions to harmonize aspects of them ... In this connection, the Council will also consider, by the end of 1993, on the basis of a report, the possibility of applying Article K.9 to such matters' (Union, European 1992).

Chapter 4

1. For a list of the members of the Reflection Group and the representatives negotiating the IGC, see Laursen (2002b: 4, 9). In contrast to the Reflection Group, the group of IGC representatives did not include members of the European Parliament.
2. For a summary of the positions of all member states at the 1996 IGC, see: http://europa.eu.int/en/agenda/igc-home/eu-doc/parlment/position/ (accessed on 25 February 2005). See also the more general discussions of member state positions in Edwards and Pijpers (1997), Hrbek (1997) and Laursen (2002a). For a discussion of the preferences of member states in the area of justice and home affairs more specifically, see Knelangen (2001: 258–264) and den Boer (2002).
3. The European Court of Justice did not propose any solutions to the deficiencies in JHA decision-making structures, as it considered this to be an inappropriate undertaking in light of the separation of powers: '[T]he Court of Justice must reconcile its concern to provide a useful contribution to the work of the Group with the duty of discretion incumbent upon it as a judicial institution' (European Court of Justice 1995: paragraph 1). It did, however, point out that its obligation to protect the rights of citizens under the first pillar was compromised by the fact that JHA, an area with potentially large implications for the rights of citizens, was excluded from the Court's jurisdiction: 'In that regard, the attention of the Intergovernmental Conference should be drawn to the legal problems which may arise in the long, or even the short, term. Thus, it is obvious that judicial protection of individuals affected by the activities of the Union, especially in the context of co-operation in the fields of Justice and Home Affairs, must be guaranteed and structured in such a way as to ensure consistent interpretation and application of both Community law and of the provisions adopted within the framework of such co-operation' (European Court of Justice 1995: paragraph 4).
4. To some extent, positing that different ideal scenarios were available at the beginning of the negotiations necessary falls prey to the fallacy of 'reading backwards'. It simplifies the messy reality of IGC negotiations insofar as the different scenarios may not have been clearly discernible at the time of negotiation, when new texts and meanings were constantly added to already existing scenarios and strategies (den Boer 2002: 522). Nevertheless, in the case of the Amsterdam IGC the preferences of member states were already relatively fixed at the start of the negotiation process (Moravcsik and Nicolaïdis 1999). As a large part of the agenda was pre-determined by Maastricht, the room for supranational entrepreneurship was generally considered to be low. Nor were there, compared to Maastricht, any significant external events that were framed in such a way as to nudge the political agenda in a different direction (Moravcsik and Nicolaïdis 1999; Beach 2002b).

5. As Ireland did not participate in Schengen, the Irish Presidency had no immediate interest in bringing Schengen within a legal-institutional framework with which it was obliged to comply.
6. See http://europa.eu.int/comm/commissioners/vitorino/index_en.htm (accessed 23 November 2004).
7. The Austrian Strategy Paper was not the first document to stress the need for an integrated approach, however. The December 1992 Edinburgh Council, confronted with refugee flows from former Yugoslavia, already agreed to address the root causes of immigration through the external policy channels of the EU (European Council 1992). Although subsequent European Councils did not come back to the issue, it was picked up again by the Commission in its 1994 communication on asylum and immigration (European Commission 1994), but again no concrete measures were taken.
8. On the intertwining of development and security, see Duffield (2001).
9. This of course leads to the question why the JHA Council agreed to the establishment of the HLWG in the first place. One explanation is that the creation of a HLWG somewhat counterbalanced the Commission, which would become a dominant actor after the communitarization of asylum and immigration policies. Institutionally, then, the creation of the HLWG could be seen as an attempt to keep some competences regarding the issue within the intergovernmental sphere, outside the influence of the Commission (van Selm 2002).
10. The most common expression of this vision is probably the idea that more police on the streets will restore trust in the public order. However, the increased visibility of the police will often trigger feelings of insecurity and contribute to the notion that something must be wrong ('why else would there be so many police?'). Moreover, if threats to the public order persist, this may fuel anxieties and fears even more ('so many police on the streets, and still we get robbed') and may, eventually, question the capacity and legitimacy of the government as the core threat manager.

Chapter 5

1. For historical accounts of the passport, see Torpey (2000), Lloyd (2003) and Gulddal and Mortensen (2004).
2. For a comparative oversight of carrier sanctions regimes in the United States and EU member states, see Cruz (1995).
3. See Hyndman (2000) for an insightful discussion of the disciplinary function of the camp and its role in the management of displacement in post-World War II humanitarian ideology.
4. Arguably, the technology of the camp as an exclusionary buffer-zone is already deployed *de facto* within many EU member states insofar as the structure of the camp can be found at the border in the form of airport holding zones and migrant detention and exit centres.
5. As 'illegality' constitutes an act of serious crime in some states but not in others, there is a large discrepancy in member state registration of

illegal aliens in the SIS. However, because all countries work from the same database, the undesirability of an alien in one state implies that the same alien is also denied access to another state. As of 1 February 2003, Italy topped the list on registering undocumented aliens with 335,306 entries, followed by Germany with 267,884 (together 77% of all entries), while Belgium (367), Denmark (147) and Iceland (10) registered least entries.

6. In 2001, British liaisons officers refused 22,515 inadequately documented immigrants to board a carrier, which is seen as 'a significant success for the network in stemming the flow of improperly documented passengers to the UK, which we intend to support and maintain' (Home Office 2002: 93). However, British Airways' Facilitation Manager (Forster 2002: 27) claims that the sanctions have encouraged the production of high quality fraudulent documents, stimulated human trafficking, while placing airline and government officials in danger.
7. See http://www.robmarine.com/indexe.html, accessed 20 April 2009. To determine the nationality of stowaways, the questionnaire includes, among others, the following questions: Where were you born?; What is your home address?; What is your religion?; Which tribe do you belong to?; Which languages do you speak?; What is your father's place of birth?; What is your father's religion?; What tribe does your father belong to?; What is the capital of your country?; What languages are spoken in your homeland?; Describe your country's flag; What crops are grown in your country?; Name any large company in your country; What is your country's currency?; What is the name of your president?; What is the name of the international airport in your homeland?; and Name any radio stations in your country.
8. On insurance as a form of governance, see the excellent work of Ericson and his colleagues (Ericson and Doyle 2003; Ericson, Doyle et al. 2003). See also Ewald (1993) and Baker and Simon (2002).
9. A preview copy of 'Coping with Stowaways' was made available to me by Videotel Marine International. The tape states that the P&I Club sustains annual losses of US$ 5 million, with single losses up to US$ 250,000 as a result of 'stowaways'.
10. See http://www.robmarine.com/indexe.html (accessed 20 April 2009).
11. See http://www.robmarine.com/indexe.html (accessed 20 April 2009).
12. See http://www.robmarine.com/indexe.html (accessed 20 April 2009).
13. Similarly, the American company DielectroKinetic Laboratories (DKL), which has developed a remote sensing device ('LifeGuard') able to detect heartbeats through various kinds of barriers has started to advertise its device (originally used for rescue missions in earthquakes, sunken ships, fires, etc.) as an effective and easy-to-manage instrument for the 'detection of stowaways in trucks and other vehicles' (http://www.dklabs.com/products.html#lifeguard1).
14. Obviously, other arguments are utilized as well. An important factor for choosing fingerprints rather than iris-scanning seems to be that the technology for the latter is in the hands of a US-based (Iridian) rather than a European company (such as Steria). While this is hinted at by the

European Commission (2003a: 5), it is more explicitly stated in the Commission's research report *Biometrics at the Frontiers: Assessing the Impact on Society*, in which the 'emergence of a vibrant European biometrics industry' is named as one of the core reasons for the introduction of biometric identification. As such a market is unlikely to emerge by itself, governments are called upon to support the industry. Interestingly, and in line with the advanced liberal motto that public intervention should be avoided, governments are portrayed here not as 'regulators' but as 'launch customers' (European Commission 2005a: 10–11).

15. As it concerns a relatively new trend, the consequences of private forms of rule are not completely mapped out and it would be interesting to examine more empirically the ways in which insurance governance operates: Do insurers constitute discriminate forms of rule favouring those who contribute to the goodness of the pool (and thus the wealth of the insurance company), while deselecting those that are not able or willing to contribute to the prevention of loss? And what are the effects of the commodification of immigration risk on the lives of undocumented immigrants who are objectified by insurance governance as an economic loss or damage?

Chapter 6

1. This reading differs from Taureck (2006) and Aradau's (2004: 389) understanding that desecuritization is an analytical category rather than a political strategy. For the Copenhagen School, (de)securitization is always a political choice.
2. For example, Wæver has identified the securitization of European integration as a responsible political act to block the 'worst' of Europe's return to its own violent past. The securitization of integration has been a powerful tool in sustaining the integration project ('if we do not integrate, then war will return!') and to promote peaceful relations between European states. For this 'good', Wæver is willing to accept the 'bad' that the EU-project is sustained through securitizing discourses in the sphere of justice and home affairs. For even if this securitizes social relations between the EU and third-country nationals, it prevents the worse scenario of a Europe returning to its past (Wæver 1995: 73–74; 2000: 285).
3. As Žižek has argued in a more Lacanian fashion, the 'multiculturalist vision-and-practice of "unity in difference" ("all equal, all different"), leaves open, as the only way to mark the Difference, the proto-sublimatory gesture of elevating a contingent Other (of race, sex, religion ...) into the absolute "Otherness" of the impossible "Thing", the ultimate threat to our identity – this Thing which must be annihilated if we are to survive' (Žižek 1999: 202).
4. In his book *Disagreement*, Rancière (1998) argues that the core of a democratic ethos is not just about the development of democratic institutions and procedures but, perhaps even more crucially, the suspension and subversion of these procedures on behalf of those who are not represented in

the social order. According to him, the first true test for democracy appeared in ancient Greece where members of the *dēmos* (those that fell outside the hierarchical matrix of society) demanded as those who are part of no part to be regarded as the point in which 'truth' and 'universality' were located. Žižek refers to another example: in the demonstrations against the communist regime in East Germany protestors shouted '*Wir* sind *das* Volk!', 'thereby performing the gesture of politicisation at its purest – they, the excluded counter revolutionary "scum" of the official Whole of the People ... claimed to stand for the people, for "all"; a couple of days later, however, the slogan changed into we are a/one people ['Wir sind ein Volk!'], clearly signalling the closure of the momentary authentic political opening' (Žižek 1999: 189). A last example – this time from popular culture – can be found in the animation movie *Antz* about a colony of ants. Whereas normally every ant has its fixed place in a colony, the film ends with a successful uprising of the worker ants against the soldier ants, with the workers exclaiming '*We* are the colony!'

Chapter 7

1. Moreover, there is thus always the possibility that certain immigrants exempted from security and control are relegated to the general risk class. For instance, if the residence permit of knowledge immigrants is not extended, they will – without any change in personal disposition – move from being a desirable economic asset to a dangerous, illegal immigrant.
2. Although there are reports of, sometimes deathly, violence against immigrants in detention centres, during exit procedures and against stowaways found on board of ship vessels (see de Stoop 1996; Fekete 2005)

Bibliography

Agamben, G. (1998). *Homo Sacer. Sovereign Power and Bare Life*. Stanford: Stanford University Press.

Agamben, G. (2002). 'Security and Terror' *Theory and Event* 5(4).

Agamben, G. (2005). *State of Exception*. Chicago: University of Chicago Press.

Ahnfelt, E. and J. From (1996). *Politisamarbeid og europeisk integrasjon. Fremveksten av justis og innenrikssamarbeid i EU, Europol og Schengen*. Oslo: Ad Notam Gyldendal.

Amnesty International (1999). *Comments by Amnesty International on the implementation of the action plans adopted by the High Level Working Group on Asylum and Migration*. Brussels: 23 December 1999.

Anderson, M., den Boer, M., Cullen, P., Gilmore, W.C., Raab, C.D. and N. Walker (1995). *Policing the European Union*. Oxford: Clarendon Press.

Andreas, P. (2000). *Border Games: Policing the US-Mexican Divide*. New York: Cornell University Press.

Aradau, C. (2001). 'Migration: The Spiral of (In)Security' *Rubrikon*, retrieved from: http://venus.ci.uw.edu.pl/~rubrikon/forum/claudia1.htm

Aradau, C. (2004). 'Security and the Democratic Scene: Desecuritization and Emancipation' *Journal of International Relations and Development* 7: 388–413.

Aradau, C. (2007). *Rethinking Trafficking in Women. Politics out of Security*. New York: Palgrave MacMillan.

Arendt, H. (1958). *The Human Condition*. Chicago: Chicago University Press.

Austrian Presidency (1998). *Strategy Paper on Immigration and Asylum Policy*. Brussels, 1 July 1998, 9809/98 CK4 27 Asim 170, retrieved from: http://www.proasyl.de/texte/europe/eu-a-o.html

Baker, T. and J. Simon, Eds. (2002). *Embracing Risk*. Chicago: Chicago University Press.

Baldwin-Edwards, M. and B. Hebenton (1994). 'Will SIS Be Europe's Big Brother?' in M. Anderson and M. den Boer, Eds, *Policing Across National Boundaries*. London: Pinter: 137–157.

Balibar, É. (2002). *Politics and the Other Scene*. London and New York: Verso.

Balibar, É. (2004). *We, The People of Europe? Reflections on Transnational Citizenship*. Princeton: Princeton University Press.

Balzacq, T. and S. Carrera (2006). 'The Hague Programme: The Long Road to Freedom, Security and Justice' in T. Balzacq and S. Carrera, Eds, *Security Versus Freedom? A Challenge for Europe's Future*. Aldershot: Ashgate: 1–34.

Barry, A. (1993). 'The European Community and European Government: Harmonization, Mobility and Space' *Economy and Society* 22(3): 314–326.

Barry, A. (1994). 'Harmonization and the Art of European Government' in C. Rootes and H. Davis, Eds, *A New Europe? Social Change and Political Transformation*. London: UCL Press: 39–54.
Barry, A. (2001). *Political Machines. Governing Technological Societies*. London: The Athlone Press.
Bauman, Z. (1998). *Globalization. The Human Consequences*. Cambridge: Polity Press.
Bauman, Z. (2004). *Wasted Lives. Modernity and Its Outcasts*. Cambridge: Polity Press.
BBC News (2003). EU Sea Patrols Target Illegal Immigrants, retrieved from: http://news.bbc.co.uk/1/hi/world/europe/2703877.stm
Beach, D. (2002a). *Bringing Negotiations back into the Study of European Integration: How Negotiations Affect the Ability of Supranational Actors to Gain Influence in IGC's*. Odense: University of Southern Denmark Press.
Beach, D. (2002b). 'Negotiating the Amsterdam Treaty: When Theory Meets Reality' in F. Laursen, Ed., *The Amsterdam Treaty. National Preference Formation, Interstate Bargaining and Outcome*. Odense: University of Southern Denmark: 593–638.
Benyon, J. (1996). 'The Politics of Police Co-ordination in the European Union' *International Journal of the Sociology of Law* 24: 353–379.
Benyon, J., Turnbull, L., Willis, A. and R. Woodward (1994). 'Understanding Police Cooperation in Europe: Setting a Framework for Analysis' in M. Anderson and M. den Boer, Eds, *Policing Across National Boundaries*. London: Pinter: 46–65.
Benyon, J., Turnbull, L., Willis, A., Woodward, R. and A. Beck (1993). *Police Co-operation in Europe: An Investigation*. Leicester: Centre for the Study of Public Order.
Bigo, D. (1994). 'The European Internal Security Field: States and Rivalries in a Newly Developing Area of Police Intervention' in M. den Boer and M. Anderson, Eds, *Policing Across National Boundaries*. London: Pinter: 161–173.
Bigo, D. (1996). *Polices en réseaux: L'expérience européenne*. Paris: Presses de Sciences Po.
Bigo, D. (2001). 'The Möbius Ribbon of Internal and External Securit(ies)' in M. Albert, D. Jacobsen and Y. Lapid, EDs, *Identities, Borders, Orders. Rethinking International Relations Theory*, Minneapolis: University of Minnesota Press: 91–116.
Bigo, D. (2002). 'Security and Immigration: Toward a Critique of the Governmentality of Unease' *Alternatives* 27: 63–92.
Bigo, D. (2006). 'Liberty, Whose Liberty? The Hague Programme and the Conception of Freedom' in T. Balzacq and S. Carrera, Eds, *Security versus Freedom? A Challenge to Europe's Future*. Aldershot: Ashgate: 35–44.
Bigo, D. and E. Guild (2004). 'Distancering af de fremmede' *Tidsskriftet Politik* 3(7).

Blair, T. (2003). *Letter to His Excellency Mr Costas Simitis: New International Approaches to Asylum Processing and Protection* 10 March, retrieved from: http://www.statewatch.org/news/2003/apr/blair-simitis-asile.pdf

Bonnefoi, S. (1994). *Europe et sécurité intérieure. Trevi – Union Européenne – Schengen*. Paris: Delmas.

Bostock, D. (2002). 'Coreper Revisited' *Journal of Common Market Studies* 40(2): 215–234.

Boswell, C. (2003a). *European Migration Policies in Flux. Changing Patterns of Inclusion and Exclusion*. London: Chatham House Papers, The Royal Institute of International Affairs, Blackwell.

Boswell, C. (2003b). 'The "External Dimension" of EU Immigration and Asylum Policy' *International Affairs* 79(3): 619–638.

Bull, H. (1977). *The Anarchical Society: A Study of order in World Politics*. London: MacMillan.

Bunyan, T. (1991). 'Towards an Authoritarian European State' *Race & Class* 32(3): 19–30.

Busch, H. (1989). 'Schengen-Gruppe. Keine Öffnung der Grenzen, dafür "Ausgleichsmaßnahmen"' *Bürgerrrechte und Polizei/CILIP* 33: 95–103.

Busch, H. (1999). *Polizeiliche Drogenbekämpfung – eine internationale Verstrikkung*. Münster: Verlag Westfälisches Dampfboot.

Butler, J. (2003). 'What is Critique? An Essay on Foucault's Virtue' *Working Paper, Kadish Center for Morality, Law & Public Affairs*, retrieved from: http://www.law.berkeley.edu/centers/kadish/what%20is%20critique%20J%20Butler.pdf

Buzan, B., Wæver, O. and J. de Wilde (1998). *Security. A New Framework for Analysis*. London: Rienner.

Callaway, S. and B. Martin. (1998). 'Papers for All Sans-Papiers in Europe' retrieved from: http://www.bok.net/pajol/sanspap/blackwomen/blackwomen3.en.html

Callovi, G. (1992). 'Regulation of Immigration in 1993: Pieces of the European Community Jig-Saw Puzzle' *International Migration Review* 26(2): 353–372.

Carrera, S. and E. Guild (2006). 'No Constitutional Treaty? Implications for the Area of Freedom, Security and Justice' in T. Balzacq and S. Carrera, Eds, *Security Versus Freedom? A Challenge for Europe's Future*. Aldershot: Ashgate: 223–240.

Chimni, B.S. (1998). 'The Geopolitics of Refugee Studies: A View from the South' *Journal of Refugee Studies* 11(4): 350–374.

Christiansen, T., Jorgensen, K.E. and A. Wiener (2001). *The Social Construction of Europe*. London: Sage.

Cissé, M. (1997). *The Sans-Papiers: The New Movement of Asylum Seekers and Immigrants without Papers in France: A Woman Draws the First Lesson*. London: Crossroads.

Cissé, M. (1999). The World of the People without Papers, retrieved from: http://www.lolapress.org/artenglish/cisse16.htm

Cissé, M. (2003). Interview with Madgiguène de Cissé, retrieved from: http://1libertaire.free.fr/madjiguen.htm

Cloos, J., Reinisch, G., Vignes, D. and J. Weyland (1993). *Le traité de Maastricht. Genèse, analyse, commentaires*. Bruxelles: Établissements Émile Bruylant.

Coordinators' Group (1989). *A Report to the European Council by the Coordinators' Group on the Free Movement of Persons ('Palma Document')*. Madrid, 15 June.

Coordinators' Group (1992). *Report to the European Council in Edinburgh from the Coordinators' Group on the Free Movement of Persons*. 3 December.

Corbett, R. (1993). *The Treaty of Maastricht. From Conception to Ratification: A Comprehensive Reference Guide*: Harlow: Longman.

Coreper (1999). *Terms of Reference of the High Level Working Group on Asylum and Migration; Preparation of Action Plans for the Most Important Countries of Origin and Transit of Asylum-seekers and Migrants*. Brussels, 22 January, 5264/2/99 Rev 2 Limite JAI 1 AG 1.

Council of the European Union (1995). *Rapport du Conseil sur le fonctionnement du TUE*. Brussels, retrieved from: http://europa.eu.int/en/agenda/igc-home/eu-doc/council/conseil.html

Council of the European Union (2004). *Regulation Establishing a Programme for Financial and Technical Assistance to Third Countries in the Areas of Migration and Asylum (AENEAS)* published in Official Journal of the European Union on 18 March 2004, L 80/1, par. (7). Brussels, 10 March, OJ 491/2004.

Crawford, A. (2002). 'The Governance of Crime and Insecurity in an Anxious Age: The Trans-European and the Local' in A. Crawford, Ed., *Crime and Insecurity. The Governance of Safety in Europe*. Portland: Willian Publishing: 27–51.

Cruz, A. (1995). *Shifting Responsibility. Carriers' Liability in the Member States of the European Union and North America*. London: Trentham Books.

De Genova, N.P. (2002). 'Migrant "Illegality" and Deportability in Everyday Life' *Annual Review of Anthropology* 31: 419–447.

de Lobkowicz, W. (1994). 'Intergovernmental Cooperation in the Field of Migration – From the Single European Act to Maastricht' in J. Monar and R. Morgan, Eds, *The Third Pillar of the European Union, Cooperation in the Fields of Justice and Home Affairs*. Brussels: European Interuniversity Press: 99–122.

de Lobkowicz, W. (2002). *L'Europe et la sécurité intérieure. Une elaboration par étapes*. Paris: La documentation française.

de Stoop, Chris (1996). *Haal de was maar binnen. Aziza of een verhaal van deportatie in Europa*. Amsterdam: De bezige bij.

de Wilde, J. (2005). 'The Environmental Sector' *Paper presented at the Inter-University Workshop on Sovereignty & Security (23 June)* Vrije universiteit, Amsterdam.

Dean, M. (2002). 'Liberal Government and Authoritarianism' *Economy and Society* 31(1): 37–61.

Dean, M. (2007). *Governing Societies. Political Perspectives on Domestic and International Rule*. New York: Open University Press.

den Boer, M. (2002). 'A New Area of Freedom, Security and Justice: The Shaping of a Hybrid Compromise' in F. Laursen, Ed., *The Amsterdam Treaty. National*

Preference Formation, Interstate Bargaining and Outcome. Odense: University of Southern Denmark Press: 509–536.

den Boer, M. and L. Corrado (2000). 'For the Record or Off the Record: Comments About the Incorporation of Schengen into the EU' *European Journal of Migration and Law* 1: 397–418.

Der Derian, J. (1987). *On Diplomacy. A Genealogy of Western Estrangement*. Oxford: Blackwell.

Der Derian, J. (1992). *Antidiplomacy: Spies, Terror, Speed, and War*. Oxford: Blackwell.

Diken, B. and C.B. Laustsen (2005). *The Culture of Exception. Sociology Facing the Camp*. London and New York: Routledge.

Doutriaux, Y. (1992). *Le traité sur l'Union Européenne*. Paris: Armand Colin.

Dublin Convention (1990). *Convention Determining the State Responsible for Examining Applications for Asylum Lodged in One of the Member States of the European Communities*. OJ C 254, 19/08/1997, retrieved from: http://europa.eu.int/infonet/library/a/97c25401/en.htm

Duff, A., Pinder, J. and R. Pryce (1994). *Maastricht and Beyond: Building the European Union*. London and New York: Routledge.

Duffield, M. (2001). *Global Governance and the New Wars. The Merging of Development and Security*. London and New York: Zed Books.

Dutch Delegation to the Council (1998). *Note from the Dutch Delegation: Task Force on Asylum and Migration*. Brussels, 23 November, 13344/98 JAI 37 AG 15.

Edwards, G. and A. Pijpers, Eds. (1997). *The Politics of European Treaty Reform. The 1996 Intergovernmental Conference and Beyond*. London: Pinter.

Ericson, R. (2007). *Crime in an Insecure World*. Cambridge: Polity Press.

Ericson, R. and A. Doyle (2003). 'Risk and Morality' in R. Ericson and A. Doyle, Eds, *Risk and Morality*. Toronto: University of Toronto Press: 1–21.

Ericson, R., Doyle, A. and D. Barry (2003). *Insurance as Governance*. Toronto: University of Toronto Press.

Ericson, R. and Kevin H. (1997). *Policing the Risk Society*. Oxford: Clarendon Press.

Eriksson, J. (2001). 'Introduction' in J. Eriksson, Ed., *Threat Politics. New Perspectives on Security, Risk and Crisis Management*. Aldershot: Ashgate: 21–37.

Esders, E. (1995). 'The European Parliament's Committee on Civil Liberties and Internal Affairs – The Committee Responsible for Justice and Home Affairs' in R. Bieber and J. Monar, Eds, *Justice and Home Affairs in the European Union. The Development of the Third Pillar*. Brussels: European Interuniversity Press: 259–276.

EU Council (1995). *Council Regulation (EC) No 1683/95 of 29 may 1995 laying down a uniform format for visas*. Brussels, OJ L 179.

EU Council (2001). *Directive 2001/51/EC supplementing the provisions of Article 26 of the Convention implementing the Schengen Agreement of 14 June 1985*, OJ L 187/45-6.28.

EU Council (2002a). *Common Consular Instructions on visas for the diplomatic missions and consular posts*. Brussels, 16 December 2002, OJ C 313.

EU Council (2002b). *Council Decision of 12 July 2002 on the adaptation of parts III and VIII of the common consular instructions.* Brussels, 16 July 2002, OJ L 187.

EU Council (2002c). *Council Directive 2002/90/EC defining the facilitation of unauthorised entry, transit and residence.* Brussels, 28 November 2002, OJ L 328/17.

EU Council (2002d). *Council Regulation (EC) No 334/2002 of 18 February 2002 amending Regulation (EC) No 1683/95 laying down a uniform format for visas.* Brussels, OJ L53/7.

EU Council (2002e). *EU Schengen Catalogue. External borders control, Removal and readmission: Recommendations and best practices.* Brussels, February 2002.

EU Council (2002f). *Proposal for a comprehensive plan to combat illegal immigration and trafficking of human beings in the European Union.* Brussels, 27 February 2002, OJ 6621/1/02 REV 1

EU Council (2003a). *Centres chargés des frontières maritimes.* Brussels, 24 October 2003, 13918/03.

EU Council (2003b). *Feasibility study on the control of the European Union's maritime borders – Final report.* Brussels, 19 September 2003, 11490/1/03 REV 1.

EU Council (2003c). *International Airports Plan – Air Borders Centre Project (Italy).* Brussels, 13 October 2003, 13524/03

EU Council (2003d). *Report of the 6th meeting of the participants of the Centre for Land Borders (CLB).* Brussels, 17 October 2003, 12799/03.

EU Council (2004). *Council Regulation No 2007/2004 Establishing a European Agency for the Management of Operational Cooperation at the External Borders of the Member States of the European Union,*, Brussels, OJL 349/1.

European Commission (1985). *Decision setting up a prior communication and consultation procedure between member states.* Brussels, 19 August 1985, OJ L 217.

European Commission (1991a). *Communication from the Commission to the Council and the European Parliament on the right of asylum.* Brussels: SEC(91) 1857 final, 11 October 1991.

European Commission (1991b). *Communication to the Council and the European Parliament on Immigration.* Brussels: SEC(91) 1855 final, 23 October 1991.

European Commission (1994). *Communication from the Commission to the Council and the European Parliament on Immigration and Asylum Policies.* COM (94) 23 Final.

European Commission (1995). *Report on the Operation of the Treaty on European Union.* Brussels, retrieved from: http://europa.eu.int/en/agenda/igc-home/eu-doc/commissn/reports.html

European Commission (1996). *Reinforcing Political Union and Preparing for Enlargement.* Brussels, retrieved from: http://europa.eu.int/en/agenda/igc-home/eu-doc/commissn/avis-en.html

European Commission (1999). *Designing Tomorrow's Commission. A Review of the Commission's Organisation and Operation.* Brussels, 7 July, retrieved from http://europa.eu.int/comm/reform/decode/screening_en.pdf

European Commission (2001). *Communication from Commissioner Vitorino to the Commission on Framework for Preparatory Actions, Budget Line 'Cooperation with third countries in the area of migration (B7-667)*. Brussels, 28 September.

European Commission (2002). *Communication from the Commission to the Council and the European Parliament. Integrating Migration Issues in the European Union's Relations with Third Countries*. Brussels, 3 December, COM(2002) 703 Final.

European Commission (2003a). *Proposal for a Council Regulation amending Regulation (EC) 1683/95 laying down a uniform format for visas [and] Proposal for a Council Regulation amending Regulation (EC) 1030/2002 laying down a uniform format for residence permits for third-country nationals*. Brussels, 24 September, COM(2003)558 final.

European Commission (2003b). *Study on the feasibility of processing asylum claims outside the EU against the background of the common European asylum system and the goal of a common asylum procedure*. Brussels, March.

European Commission (2004). *Communication from the Commission to the Council and the European Parliament on the managed entry in the EU of persons in need of international protection and the enhancement of the protection capacity of the regions of origin – 'Improving Access to Durable Solutions'* Brussels, 4 June, Com(2004) 410 final.

European Commission (2005a). *Biometrics at the Frontiers: Assessing the impact on Society. For the European Parliament Committee on Citizens' Freedoms and Rights, Justice and Home Affairs (LIBE)*. Brussels, EUR 21585 EN.

European Commission (2005b). *Justice, Freedom and Security from a European Commission perspective*, retrieved from: http://europa.eu.int/comm/dgs/justice_home/index_en.htm

European Council (1988). *Rhodes European Council: Presidency Conclusions*. December.

European Council (1989). *Strasbourg European Council: Presidency Conclusions*. 9 December.

European Council (1990). *Dublin European Council: Presidency Conclusions*. 26 June.

European Council (1992). *Edinburgh European Council: Presidency Conclusions*. 11–12 December.

European Council (1994). *Corfu European Council: Presidency Conclusions*: 24–25 June.

European Council (1995a). *Cannes European Council: Presidency Conclusions*: 15–16 December.

European Council (1995b). *Madrid European Council: Presidency Conclusions*. Madrid, 15–16 December.

European Council (1996a). *Dublin European Council: Presidency Conclusions*. 13–14 December.

European Council (1996b). *Florence European Council: Presidency Conclusions*. 21–22 June.

European Council (1998a). *Action Plan of the Council and Commission on how best to implement the provisions of the Amsterdam Treaty establishing an*

area of freedom, security and justice. Brussels, 4 December, retrieved from: http://www.statewatch.org/semdoc/database/aponAFSJ.html
European Council (1998b). *Cardiff European Council: Presidency Conclusions*. 15–16 June.
European Council (1999). *Tampere European Council: Presidency Conclusions*. 15–16 October.
European Council (2001). *Laeken European Council: Presidency Conclusions*: 14–15 December 2001.
European Council (2002). *Seville European Council: Presidency Conclusion*: 21–22 June 2002.
European Council (2003). *Thessaloniki European Council: Presidency Conclusions*: 19/20 June.
European Court of Justice (1987). Joined Cases 281, 283 to 285 and 287/5. Brussels, ECR (3230).
European Court of Justice (1995). *Report of the Court of Justice on Certain Aspects of the Application of the Treaty on European Union*. Luxembourg, May 1995, retrieved from: http://europa.eu.int/en/agenda/igc-home/eu-doc/justice/cj_rep.html
European Parliament (1987). *Resolution on the right of asylum*, Committee on Legal Affairs and Citizens' Rights, Doc. B2-512/87, 18 June.
European Parliament (1992). *Opinion for the Committee on the Rules of procedure, the verification of Credentials and Immunities on the amendments to be made to the Rules of procedure as a result of the Treaty on European Union (rapporteur J.M. Lafuente Lopez)*. Brussels: PE 202.365, 6 October.
European Parliament (1993a). *Draft inter-institutional agreement between the European Parliament, the Council and the Commission on the procedure for implementing Title VI of the Treaty on European Union* Brussels: PE 207.086/rev, 1 December.
European Parliament (1993b). *Report of the Committee on Civil Liberties and Internal Affairs on cooperation in the fields of justice and home affairs under the Treaty on European Union (Title VI and other provisions) (rapporteur C. Robles Piquer)*. Brussels: PE A3-0215/93, 1 July.
European Parliament (1995). *Resolution from 17 May 1995 on the functioning of the Treaty on European Union with a view to the Intergovernmental Conference 1996* Brussels: OJ C 151, 19 June.
European Parliament (1996). *Resolution on the Opinion of the European Parliament on the Calling of the IGC 1996 and on the assessment of the work by the Reflection Group and on the establishment of the political priorities of the European Parliament with a view to the IGC 1996* Brussels, 13 March.
European Parliament (1997). *The 1996 IGC and the Effectiveness of the Union*. Briefing No. 25, 5 March, retrieved from: http://www.europarl.eu.int/igc1996/fiches/fiche25_en.htm
European Parliament (2000a). *Report on asylum-seekers and migrants – action plans for countries of origin and transit (rapporteur J. S. Hernandez Mollar)* Brussels: PE A5-0057/2000 Final, 29 February.

European Parliament (2000b). *Report on the Draft Action Plan for Albania and neighbouring regions (rapporteur: A. Karamanou)* Brussels: PE A5-0287/2000 Final, 12 October.

European Union (1992). *Treaty on European Union,* accessible at: http://europa.eu/eur-lex/en/treaties/dat/EU_treaty.html

European Union (2002). *Consolidated Version of the Treaty on European Union.* 24 December 2002, Brussels, retrieved from: http://europa.eu.int/eur-lex/lex/en/treaties/dat/12002M/pdf/12002M_EN.pdf

Ewald, F. (1993). *Der Omsorgestaat.* Franfurt am Main: Suhrkamp.

Fekete, L. (2005). *The Deportation Machine: Europe, Asylum and Human Rights.* European Race Bulletin 51, Institute of Race Relations, London.

Forster, J. (2002). 'Sanctions Imposed on Carriers: Impact on Migration Flows and Asylum Requests' in C. Faria, Ed., *Managing Migration Flows and Preventing Illegal Immigration,* Maastricht: EIPA: 25–28.

Fortescue, J.A. (1995). 'First Experiences with the Implementation of the Third Pillar Provisions' in J. Monar and R. Bieber, Eds, *Justice and Home Affairs in the European Union. The Development of the Third Pillar,* Brussels: European Interuniversity Press: 19–28.

Fortescue, J.A. (2002). 'Préface' in W. de Lobkowicz, Ed., *L'Europe et la sécurité intérieure. Une elaboration par étapes,* Paris: La documentation française: 7–14.

Foucault, M. (2000a). "'Omnes et Singulatim": Toward a Critique of Political Reason' in J.D. Faubion, Ed., *Essential Works of Foucault 1954–1984: Volume 3, Power.* London: Penguin Books: 298–325.

Foucault, M. (2000b). 'Space, Knowledge, and Power' in J.D. Faubion, Ed., *Essential Works of Foucault 1954–1984: Volume 3, Power.* London: Penguin Books: 349–364.

France/Germany (1990a). *Kohl-Mitterand Letter to the Irish Presidency*: Agence Europe, 20 April.

France/Germany (1990b). *Kohl-Mitterand Letter to the Italian Presidency*: Agence Europe, 10-11 December.

Freeman, G. (1995). 'Modes of Immigration Politics in Liberal Democratic States' *International Migration Review* 29(4): 881–902.

Geddes, A. (2000). *Immigration and European Integration. Towards Fortress Europe?* Manchester: Manchester University Press.

Geddes, A. (2003). *The Politics of Migration and Immigration in Europe.* London: Sage.

Gordon, C. (1991). 'Governmental Rationality: An Introduction' in G. Burchell, C. Gordon and P. Miller, Eds, *The Foucault Effect. Studies in Governmentality,* Chicago: Chicago University Press: 1–52.

Guild, E. (2004). 'The Borders of the European Union: Visas and Carriers Sanctions' *Tidsskriftet Politik,* 3(7):

Guild, E. and J. Niessen (1996). *The Developing Immigration and Asylum Policies of the European Union. Adopted Conventions, Resolutions, Recommendations, Decisions and Conclusions.* The Hague: Kluwer Law International.

Guiraudon, V. (2000). 'European Integration and Migration Policy: Vertical Policy-making as Venue Shopping' *Journal of Common Market Studies* 38(2): 251–271.

Guiraudon, V. (2001). 'De-nationalizing Control. Analyzing State Responses to Constraints on Migration Control' in V. Guiraudon and C. Joppke, Eds, *Controlling a New Migration World*. London and New York: Routledge: 31–64.

Guiraudon, V. and G. Lahav (2000). 'A Reappraisal of the State Sovereignty Debate: The Case of Migration Control' *Comparative Political Studies* 33(2): 163–195.

Gulddal, J. and M. Mortensen, Eds. (2004). *Pas. Identitet, kultur og grænser*. Copenhagen: Informations forlag.

Guyomarch, A. (1997). 'Cooperation in the Fields of Policing and Judicial Affairs' in S. Stavridis, E. Mossialos, R. Morgan and H. Machin, Eds, *New Challenges to the European Union: Policies and Policy-Making*. Dartmouth: Aldershot: 123–150.

Hassner, P. (1998). 'Refugees: A Special Case for Cosmopolitan Citizenship?' in D. Archibugi, D. Held and M. Koehler, Eds, *Re-imagining Political Community. Studies in Cosmopolitan Democracy*. Cambridge: Polity Press: 273–286.

Hayter, T. (2004). *Open Borders. The Case against Immigration Controls*. London: Pluto Press.

Hebenton, B. and T. Thomas (1995). *Policing Europe. Co-operation, Conflict and Control*. New York: St. Martin's Press.

Heukels, T. and J. de Zwaan (1994). 'The Configuration of the European Union: Community Dimensions of Institutional Interaction' in D. Curtin and T. Heukels, Eds, *Institutional Dynamics of European Integration: Essays in Honour of Henry G. Schermers*. Dordrecht: Martinus Nijhoff Publishers: 195–228.

Hindess, B. (1996). *Discourses of Power. From Hobbes to Foucault*. Oxford: Blackwell.

Hix, S. (1999). *The Political System of the European Union*. New York: St. Martin's Press.

Hollifield, J. (1992). *Immigrants, Markets and States: The Political Economy of Post-War Europe*. Cambridge: Cambridge University Press.

Hollifield, J. (1994). 'Immigration and Republicanism in France: Searching for the Hidden Consensus' in W. Cornelius, P. Martin and J. Hollifield, Eds, *Controlling Immigration: A Global Perspective*. Stanford: Stanford University Press.

Home Office (2002). *Secure Borders, Safe Haven. Integration with Diversity in Modern Britain*. Retrieved from: http://www.official-documents.co.uk/document/cm53/5387/cm5387.pdf

Home Office (2003). *A New Vision for Refugees. Final Report*. 5 February.

Hrbek, R., Ed. (1997). *Die Reform der Europäischen Union. Positionen und Perspektiven anläßlich der Regierungskonferenz*. Baden-Baden: Nomos Verlagsgesellschaft.

Huysmans, J. (1995). 'Migrants as a Security Problem: Dangers of "Securitizing" Societal Issues' in R. Miles and D. Thränhardt, Eds, *Migration and*

European Integration: The Dynamics of Inclusion and Exclusion. London: Pinter: 53–72.

Huysmans, J. (1998). 'The Question of the Limit: Desecuritisation and the Aesthetics of Horror in Political Realism' *Millennium* 27(3): 569–589.

Huysmans, J. (2000a). 'The European Union and the Securitization of Migration' *Journal of Common Market Studies* 38(5): 751–777.

Huysmans, J. (2000b). 'Contested Community. Migration and the Question of the Political in the EU' in M. Kelstrup and M.C. Williams, Eds, *International Relations Theory and the Politics of European Integration. Power, Security and Community*. London and New York: Routledge: 149–170.

Huysmans, J. (2004a). 'A Foucaultian View on Spill-Over: Freedom and Security in the EU' *Journal of International Relations and Development* 7: 294–318.

Huysmans, J. (2004b). 'Minding Exceptions. Politics of Insecurity and Liberal Democracy' *Contemporary Political Theory* 3(3): 321–341.

Huysmans, J. (2006). *The Politics of Insecurity. Fear, Migration and Asylum in the EU*. London and New York: Routledge.

Hyndman, J. (2000). *Managing Displacement. Refugees and the Politics of Humanitarianism*. Minneapolis: University of Minnesota Press.

Institute of Race Relations (2004). *Migration News Sheet*. London, November.

Irish Presidency (1996). *The European Union Today and Tomorrow. Adapting the European Union for the Benefit of Its Peoples and Preparing It for the Future (Dublin II)*. Brussels, 5 December, CONF 2500/96.

Isin, E. (2000). *Being Political. Genealogies of Citizenship*. Minneapolis: University of Minnesota Press.

Isin, E. (2004). 'The Neurotic Citizen' *Citizenship Studies* 8(3): 217–235.

JHA Council (1999). *JHA Council Meeting*. 2 December.

Jobard, F. (1999). 'Schengen ou le désordre des causes' *Vacarme*, retrieved from: http://vacarme.eu.org/article19.html

Jørgensen, K.E., Ed. (1997). *Reflective Approaches to European Governance*. Basingstoke: Palgrave MacMillan.

Jutila, M. (2006). 'Desecuritizing Minority Rights: Against Determinism' *Security Dialogue* 37(2): 167–185.

Knelangen, W. (2001). *Das Politikfeld innere Sicherheit im Integrationsprozess. Die Entstehung einer Europäischen Politik der inneren Sicherheit*. Opladen: Leske and Budrich.

Kristeva, J. (1982). *Powers of Horror. An Essay on Abjection*. Columbia: Columbia University Press.

Kruijtbosch, E.D.J. (1993). 'Benelux Experiences in the Abolition of Border Controls' in H.G. Schermers, C. Flinterman, A.E. Kellermann, J.C. van Haersholte and G.-W. A. van de Meent, Eds, *Free Movement of Persons in Europe*. Dordrecht: Martinus Nijhoff Publishers: 31–40.

Kymlicka, W. (2005). *Multicultural Citizenship*. Oxford: Clarendon Press.

Laclau, E. and C. Mouffe (1990). 'Post-Marxism without Apologies' in E. Laclau, Ed., *New Reflections on the Revolution of Our Time*. London and New York: Verso: 97–132.

Lahav, G. (1998). 'Immigration and the State: The Devolution and Privatisation of Immigration Control in the EU' *Journal of Ethnic and Migration Studies* 24(4): 675–694.

Lahav, G. (2004a). *Immigration and Politics in the New Europe. Reinventing Borders.* Cambridge: Cambridge University Press.

Lahav, G. (2004b). 'Public Opinion toward Immigration in the European Union. Does It Matter?' *Comparative Political Studies* 37(10): 1151–1183.

Laursen, F. (1997). 'The Lessons of Maastricht' in G. Edwards and A. Pijpers, Eds, *The Politics of European Treaty Reform. The 1996 Intergovernmental Conference and Beyond.* London: Pinter: 59–73.

Laursen, F., Ed. (2002a). *The Amsterdam Treaty: National Preference Formation, Interstate Bargaining and Outcome.* Odense: Odense University Press.

Laursen, F. (2002b). 'Introduction: Overview of the 1996–1997 Intergovernmental Conference (IGC) and the Treaty of Amsterdam' in: F. Laursen, Ed., *The Amsterdam Treaty. National Preference Formation, Interstate Bargaining and Outcome.* Odense: University of Southern Denmark Press: 1–22.

Laursen, F. and S. Vanhoonacker, Eds. (1992). *The Intergovernmental Conference on Political Union. Institutional Reforms, New Policies and International Identity of the European Community.* Maastricht: European Institute for Public Administration.

Laursen, F. Vanhoonacker, S. and R. Wester (1992). 'Overview of the Negotiations' in F. Laursen and S. Vanhoonacker, Eds, *The Intergovernmental Conference on Political Union. Institutional Reforms, New Policies and International Identity of the European Community.* Maastricht: European Institute for Public Administration: 3–24.

Lavenex, S. (2001). *The Europeanisation of Refugee Policies. Between Human Rights and Internal Security.* Aldershot: Ashgate.

Leander, A. (2005a). 'African States and the Market for Force: The Destabilizing Concequences of Private Military Companies' *Journal for Peace Research* 42(5): 605–622.

Leander, A. (2005b). 'The Power to Construct International Security: On the Significance of Private Military Companies' *Millennium* 33(3): 803–826.

Lewis, J. (1998). 'Is the 'Hard Bargaining' Image of the Council Misleading? The Committee of Permanent Representatives and the Local Elections Directive' *Journal of Common Market Studies* 36(4): 479–504.

Lewis, J. (2000). 'The Methods of Community in EU Decision-Making and Administrative Rivalry in the Council's Infrastructure' *Journal of European Public Policy* 7(2): 261–289.

Lippert, R. (1999). 'Governing Refugees: The Relevance of Governmentality to Understanding the International Refugee Regime' *Alternatives* 24(3): 391–432.

Lisle, D. (2003). 'Site Specific. Medi(t)ations at the Airport' in F. Debrix and C. Weber, Eds, *Rituals of Mediation. International Politics and Social Meaning.* Minneapolis: Minnesota University Press: 3–29.

Lloyd, M. (2003). *The Passport. The History of Man's Most Travelled Document.* Sutton: Phoenix Mill.

Lodge, J. (2002). 'Freedom, Security and Justice: Pillar III and Protecting the "Internal Acquis"' in A. Crawford, Ed., *Crime and Insecurity. The Governance of Safety in Europe*. Portland: Willian Publishing: 102–134.

Loescher, G. and J. Milner (2003). 'The "Missing Link": The Need for Comprehensive Engagement in Regions of Refugee Origin' *International Affairs* 79(3): 595–618.

Lyon, D. (2003). *Surveillance After September 11*. Cambridge: Polity Press.

Martiniello, M. (1995). 'European Citizenship, European Identity, and Migrants: Towards the Post-national State?' in R. Miles and D. Thränhardt, Eds, *Migration and European Integration: The Dynamics of Inclusion and Exclusion*. London: Pinter: 37–52.

Miles, R. (1999). 'Analysing the Political Economy of Migration: The Airport as an "Effective" Institution of Control' in A. Brah, M.J Hickman and M. Mac an Ghail, Eds, *Global Futures: Migration, Environment and Globalization*. Basingstoke: MacMillan: 161–183.

Ministerie van Buitenlandse Zaken (1999). *Brief van de Staatssecretaris van Buitenlandse Zaken aan de Voorzitter van de Tweede Kamer der Staten-Generaal*. The Hague, 19 February 1999, DCP/JP-081/99/19 326, No. 214.

Mitsilegas, V., Monar, J. and W. Rees (2003). *The European Union and Internal Security: Guardian of the People?* Basingstoke: Palgrave MacMillan.

Monar, J. (1995). 'Democratic Control of Justice and Home Affairs: The European Parliament and the National Parliaments' in R. Bieber and J. Monar, Eds, *Justice and Home Affairs in the European Union. The Development of the Third Pillar*. Brussels: European Interuniversity Press: 243–258.

Monar, J. (1997). 'European Union – Justice and Home Affairs: A Balance Sheet' in G. Edwards and A. Pijpers, Eds, *The Politics of European Treaty Reform. The 1996 Intergovernmental Conference and Beyond*. London: Pinter: 326–339.

Monar, J. (2000). 'Justice and Home Affairs' *Journal of Common Market Studies* 38(Annual Review): 125–142.

Monar, J. (2001). 'The Dynamics of Justice and Home Affairs: Laboratories, Driving Factors and Costs' *Journal of Common Market Studies* 39(4): 747–764.

Monar, J. (2002). 'Institutionalizing Freedom, Security, and Justice' in J.n Peterson and M. Shackleton, Eds, *The Institutions of the European Union*. Oxford: Oxford University Press: 187–209.

Moravcsik, A. (1998). *The Choice for Europe: Social Purpose and State Power from Messina to Maastricht*. New York: Cornell University Press.

Moravcsik, A. and K. Nicolaïdis (1998). 'Keynote Article: Federal Ideals and Constitutional Realities in the Treaty of Amsterdam' *Journal of Common Market Studies* 36(Annual Review): 13–38.

Moravcsik, A. and K. Nicolaïdis (1999). 'Explaining the Treaty of Amsterdam: Interests, Influence, Institutions' *Journal of Common Market Studies* 37(1): 59–85.

Müller, T. (2003). *Die Innen- und Justizpolitik der Europäischen Union. Eine Analyse der Integrationsentwicklung*. Opladen: Leske and Budrich.

Nanz, K.-P. (1995). 'The Schengen Agreement: Preparing the Free Movement of Persons in the European Union' in R. Bieber and J. Monar, Eds, *Justice*

and Home Affairs in the European Union. The Development of the Third Pillar. Brussels: European Interuniversity Press: 29–48.
Niemeier, M. (1995). 'The K.4 Committee and Its Position in the Decision Making Process' in R. Bieber and J. Monar, Eds, *Justice and Home Affairs in the European Union. The Development of the Third Pillar.* Brussels: European Interuniversity Press: 321–332.
Niessen, J. (1999). 'International Migration on the EU Foreign Policy Agenda' *European Journal of Migration and Law* 1: 483–496.
Noll, G. (2003). 'Visions of the Exceptional: Legal and Theoretical Issues Raised by Transit Processing Centres and Protection Zones' *European Journal of Migration and Law* 5(3): 303–342.
Nyers, P. (2003). 'Abject Cosmopolitanism: the politics of protection in the anti-deportation movement' *Third World Quarterly* 24(6): 1069–1093.
Occhipinti, J.D. (2003). *The Politics of EU Police Cooperation. Toward a European FBI?* London: Lynne Riener.
Poster, M. (1996). 'Databases as Discourse, or Electronic Interpellations' in P. Heelas, S. Lash and P. Morris, Eds, *Detraditonalization. Critical Reflections on Authority and Identity.* Oxford: Blackwell: 277–293.
Rajaram, P.K. and C. Grundy-Warr (2004). 'The Irregular Migrant as Homo Sacer: Migration and Detention in Australia, Malaysia, and Thailand' *International Migration* 42(1): 33–64.
Rancière, J. (1995). *On the Shores of Politics.* London: Verso.
Rancière, J. (1998). *Disagreement.* Minneapolis: University of Minnesota Press.
Reflection Group (1995a). *Progress Report from the Chairman of the Reflection Group on the 1996 Intergovernmental Conference.* Madrid, 1 September, SN 509/1/95 REV 1 (reflex 10).
Reflection Group (1995b). *Reflection's Group Report.* Messina, 2 June, 5 December, Brussels, retrieved from: http://europa.eu.int/en/agenda/igc-home/eu-doc/reflect/final.html
Roe, P. (2004). 'Securitization and Minority Rights: Conditions of Desecuritization' *Security Dialogue* 35(3): 279–294.
Roe, P. (2006). 'Reconstructing Identities or Managing Minorities? Desecuritizing Minority Rights: A Response to Jutila' *Security Dialogue* 37(3): 425–438.
Rose, N. (1999). *Powers of Freedom. Reframing Political Thought.* Cambridge: Cambridge University Press.
Rupprecht, R. (1989). 'Wettlauf der Schnecken: Probleme und Konsequenzen des Abbaus von Grenzkontrollen' *Kriminalistik* 43: 263–270.
Rupprecht, R. (1993). 'Internationalization of Police Cooperation in Western Europe: the German Perspective' in C.J.C.F. Fijnaut, Ed., *The Internationalization of Police Cooperation in Western Europe.* Deventer: Kluwer Law and Taxation Publishers: 41–48.
Rupprecht, R. and M. Hellenthal (1992). 'Programm für eine Europäische Gemeinschaft der Inneren Sicherheit' in R. Rupprecht and M. Hellenthal, Eds, *Innere Sicherheit im Europäischen Binnenmarkt.* Gütersloh: Verlag Bertelsmann Stiftung: 23–320.

Salter, M. (2008). 'When the Exception becomes the Rule' *Citizenship Studies* 12(4): 365–380.

Sasse, G. (2005). 'Securitization or Securing Rights? Exploring the Conceptual Foundations of Policies towards Minorities and Migrants in Europe' *Journal of Common Market Studies* 43(4): 673–693.

Schengen (1994). 'Decision of the Executive Committee of 22 December 1994 Introducing and Applying the Schengen Agreements in Airports and Aerodromes' SCH7COM-ex(94)17.

Schengen Agreement (1985). *The Schengen Agreement on the Gradual Abolition of Controls at the Common Frontiers*. 14 June.

Schengen Convention (1990). *Convention Implementing the Schengen Agreement of 14 June 1985 between the Governments of States of the Benelux Economic Union, the Federal Republic of Germany and the French Republic on the Gradual Abolition of Checks at their Common Borders*, retrieved from: http://europa.eu.int/eur-lex/lex/LexUriServ/LexUriServ.do?uri=CELEX:42000A0922(02):EN:HTML.

Schmitt, C. (1996). *The Concept of the Political*. Chicago: University of Chicago Press.

Sciortino, G. (2000). 'Toward a Political Sociology of Entry Policies: Conceptual Problems and Theoretical Proposals' *Journal of Ethnic and Migration Studies* 26(2): 213–228.

Statewatch (2005). *Three Quarters of a Million 'Illegal Aliens' Banned from Schengen Area*, retrieved from: www.statewatch.org/news/2005/apr/08SISart96.htm

Steria (2003a). *Eurodac project centralizes processing of asylum applications on a European level*, retrieved from: www.steria.com/casestud/casestudies/eurodac.htm.

Steria (2003b). *The European Commission chooses Steria's Biometrics Know-how to Process Asylum Requests and Fight Illegal Immigration*, press release, 14 January, retrieved from: www.steria.com/press/releases/releaseeurodac.htm

Stetter, S. (2000). 'Regulating Migration: Authority Delegation in Justice and Home Affairs' *Journal of European Public Policy* 7(1): 80–103.

Taureck, R. (2006). 'Securitisation Theory and Securitisation Studies' *Journal of International Relations and Development* 9(1): 53–61.

The European Council for Refugees and Exiles (1999). *Guarding Standards – Shaping the Agenda. Analysis of the Treaty of Amsterdam and Present EU Policy on Migration, Asylum and Anti-Discrimination*. Brussels, May, retrieved from: http://www.ecre.org/positions/guarden.pdf

The Guardian (2003). *Hunger strike grips Belgium*. Brussels, 2 August.

The London P&I Club (2004). 'Stowaways Becoming More Inventive and Determined' *Stoploss Bulletin* 33.

The Observer (2003). *Secret Balkan Camp Built to hold UK Asylum Seekers. Britain to Ship Refugees to Croatian Army Base for 'Offshore Processing'* 15 June.

Torpey, J. (2000). *The Invention of the Passport*. Cambridge: Cambridge University Press.

Trevi (1989). *Declaration of Ministers of the Trevi Group*. Paris, 15 December.

Trevi (1990). Programme of Action relating to the reinforcement of police cooperation and of the endeavours to combat terrorism or other forms of organised crime, June.

Trevi/AHWGI (1987). *Declaration of the Belgian Presidency: Meeting of Justice and Interior Ministers of the European Community*: Brussels, 28 April.

Uçarer, E.M. (2001). 'From the Sidelines to Centre Stage: Sidekick No More? The European Commission in Justice and Home Affairs' *European Integration online Papers (EioP)* 5, retrieved from: http://eiop.or.at/eiop/texte/2001-005a.htm

Ugur, M. (1995). 'Freedom of Movement versus Exclusion: A Reinterpretation of the "Insider-Outsider" Divide in the European Union' *International Migration Review* 29(4): 964–999.

UNCHR (2003). *Asylum Applications Lodged In Industrialized Coutries: Levels and Trends, 2000-2002*, retrieved from: http://www.ecre.org/factfile/FAQfiles/unhcrind02.pdf

Valverde, M. and M. Mopas (2004). 'Insecurity and the Dream of Targeted Governance' in W. Larner and W. Walters, Eds, *Global Governmentality. Governing International Spaces*. London and New York: Routledge: 233 -250.

van de Rijt, W. (1998). 'Le fonctionnement des institutions Schengen: "Pragmatisme, toujours"' in M. den Boer, Ed., *Schengen's Final Days? The Incorporation of Schengen into the New TEU, External Borders and Information Systems*. Maastricht: European Institute of Public Administration: 59–66.

van Munster, R. and S. Sterkx (2005). 'Governing Mobility: The Externalization of European Migration Policy and the Boundaries of the European Union' in M. Haverland and R. Holzhacker, Eds, *European Research Reloaded: Cooperation and Integration among Europeanized States*. The Hague: Kluwer: 229–250.

van Selm, J. (2002). 'Immigration and Asylum or Foreign Policy: The EU's Approach to Migrants and Their Countries of Origin' in S. Lavenex and M. Uçarer, Eds, *Migration and the Externalities of European Integration*. Lanham: Lexington Book: 143–160.

Verstraete, G. (2001). 'Technological Frontiers and the Politics of Mobility in the European Union' *New Formations* 43: 26–43.

Wæver, O. (1995). 'Securitization and Desecuritization' in R. Lipschutz, Ed., *On Security*. New York: Columbia University Press: 44–86.

Wæver, O. (2000). 'The EU as a Security Actor: Reflections from a Pessimistic Constructivist on Post-sovereign Security Orders' in M. Kelstrup and M. C. Williams, Eds, *International Relations Theory and the Politics of European Integration. Power, Security and Community*. London and New York: Routledge: 250–294.

Wagner, W. (2003). 'Analysing the European Politics of Internal Security' *Journal of European Public Policy* 10(6): 1033–1039.

Wallace, W. (1999). 'The Sharing of Sovereignty: the European Paradox' *Political Studies* XLVII: 503–521.

Walters, W. (2002). 'Mapping Schengenland: Denaturalizing the Border' *Environment and Planning D* 20: 561–580.

Walters, W. and J.H. Haahr (2005). *Governing Europe. Discourse, Governmentality and European Integration*. London and New York: Routledge.
Weldes, J. (1996). 'Constructing National Interests' *European Journal of International Relations* 2(3): 275–318.
Williams, M.C. (2003). 'Words, Images, Enemies: Securitization and International Politics' *International Studies Quarterly* 47: 511–531.
Withol de Wenden, C. (1999). 'Post-Amsterdam Migration policy and European Citizenship' *European Journal of Migration and Law* 1: 89–101.
Wrench, P. (1996). 'Intergovernmental Co-operation in the Areas of Police and Justice' in K. Hailbronner, Ed., *Zusammenarbeit der Polizei- und Justizverwaltungen in Europa. Die Situation nach Maastricht – Schengen und SIS*. Heidelberg: 39–46.
Žižek, S. (1999). *The Ticklish Subject. The Absent Centre of Political Ontology*. New York and London: Verso.
Zolberg, A.R., Suhrke, A. and S. Aquayo (1989). *Escape from Violence: Conflict and the Refugee Crisis in the Developing World*. Oxford: Oxford University Press.

Index

Note: An 'n' after a page number indicates a note on that page.